The
Boston
Harbor
Islands

The Boston Harbor Islands National Park Area

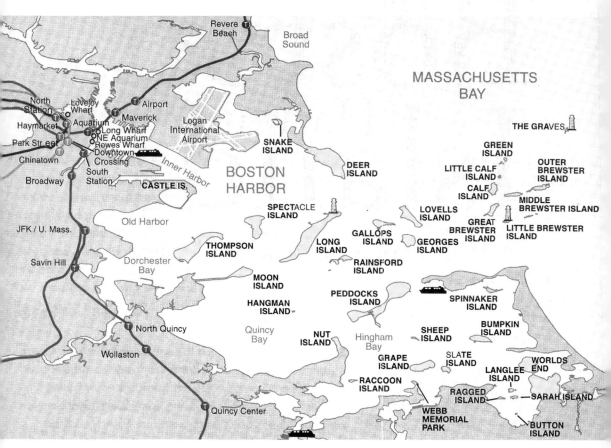

Courtesy of the National Park Service (NPS).

The Boston Harbor Islands

Harbor

The

Islands

A History of an Urban Wilderness

David Kales

Charleston London

History
PRESS

Published by The History Press
Charleston, SC 29403
www.historypress.net

Cover image: Boston Light. *Photograph courtesy of the Massachusetts Water Resources Authority.*

First published 2007

Manufactured in the United Kingdom

ISBN 978.1.59629.290.1

Library of Congress Cataloging-in-Publication Data

Kales, David.
  Boston Harbor Islands : a history of urban wilderness / David Kales.
     p. cm.
  Includes bibliographical references and index.
  ISBN 978-1-59629-290-1 (alk. paper)
  1. Boston Harbor Islands (Mass.)--History. 2. Boston Harbor Islands
(Mass.)--Environmental conditions. 3. Human ecology--Massachusetts--Boston
Harbor Islands--History. 4. Human geography--Massachusetts--Boston Harbor
Islands--History. 5. Nature--Effect of human beings
on--Massachusetts--Boston Harbor Islands--History. 6. Boston Harbor Islands
National Recreation Area (Mass.)--History. I. Title.
  F73.63.K34 2007
  974.4'6--dc22
                                   2007018235

CONTENTS

In memory of Judy Goodman and to all the friends of the Boston Harbor Islands past, present and future.

ACKNOWLEDGEMENTS

Ever since I wrote my first book on the Harbor Islands, *All About the Boston Harbor Islands*, co-authored with my wife Emily in 1976, I have met many people who have assisted me in the research and the narrative of this book. To begin with, I would like to express my gratitude to the Volunteers and Friends of the Boston Harbor Islands. Suzanne Gall Marsh, Friends founder, has shared her vision of a Boston Harbor Islands park since the time I began working on my first book. Steve Marcus, chairman of the Friends board, has been a major source of "intelligence" and networking for me on park developments. Together, they have shown me the importance of volunteerism and public participation in the stewardship of the park.

I want to thank Bruce Jacobson, superintendent, and the staff of the Boston Harbor Islands National Park Area and members of the Advisory Council to the Boston Harbor Islands Partnership, all of whom have provided information and background materials that have helped me appreciate the natural, cultural and historical resources of the park, as well as the challenging issues of park management.

Thanks also to the following: Mary Lydon, librarian, and Barbara Allen, communications specialist, at the Massachusetts Water Resources Authority, who guided me through historical records of Deer Island and provided many of the images of Boston Harbor and the islands in this book; Ellen Berkland, city of Boston archaeologist, who provided me with a number of historical and cultural reports on the islands, including Long and Rainsford Islands; the Hull Lifesaving Museum, which opened up its historical files on Calf Island and the Brewsters; the Boston Public Library and the Massachusetts Historical Society, both of which provided me with historical maps, prints and documents relating to the Boston Harbor Islands. Special thanks to Gerald Butler, who preserved many photographs of the military installations of the Harbor Islands, and has generously shared them with me since the writing of my first book.

This book is dedicated especially to Judy Goodman, who was a good friend, supporter, and with others, a tireless worker in the creation of Nut Island Park. A heartfelt thanks to her husband Ron Goodman, also my good friend and photographer who captured the images, past and present, in this book. Finally, to my wife, Emily, who began this journey through the islands with me over thirty years ago.

INTRODUCTION

Thousands of travelers fly over them daily to and from Boston, yet they know little of their existence. Few people, outside of Boston, have ever heard of them, although seven million people live within a fifty-mile radius of them. Even most Bostonians are only dimly aware of the islands of Boston Harbor. Despite their anonymity, the Boston Harbor Islands are a national park, established in 1996 by Congress to preserve and protect the natural, cultural and historic resources of a drumlin island system within Boston Harbor.

The thirty-four islands and peninsulas totaling 1,600 acres of land and covering fifty square miles of Boston Harbor that constitute the national park area hardly evoke an image of majestic mountains and vast forest wildernesses associated with our national parks. Not at first sight. Among the islands' most notable features are a wastewater treatment plant with giant cylindrical sludge digesters dominating the entrance to Boston Harbor; a reclaimed garbage dump; and several bedrock outcroppings, one of which was referred to by an energy company wanting to build a liquefied natural gas (LNG) terminal there as "a barren wasteland."

Given these jarring images, one must wonder what on earth is the national significance of this park? How did it become a national park? And why are these islands called an urban wilderness?

To answer these questions, I have cast my narrative of the Boston Harbor Islands as a history—a history that park planners say, "collectively represent an unbroken historical thread in the story of maritime and urban development."

It is a history of islands on the edge—on the edge of the continent, where a drumlin field intersects a coastline (a geological rarity) and where land meets sea. With the growth of Boston, the islands came to be unique for their lack of human habitation and development at the edge of a major metropolitan area. And over the centuries, the islands have been on the edge of society's places to isolate institutions, activities and people—"the unwashed and unwanted."

The islands have been home in the harbor, not only to a rich diversity of plant and animal life for hundreds of millenniums, but to Native Americans who lived on them for several thousand years before the white man came. With the discovery of the New World, the islands became a portal, marking the maritime entry to New England and playing an important role in European exploration, navigation, commerce and defense.

The challenge of navigating through Boston Harbor led to the construction of the country's first lighthouse (still in operation), Boston Light on Little Brewster Island. Fort Warren on Georges Island, Fort Independence on Castle Island and remnants of many other fortifications on islands throughout the harbor remain as monuments to the strategic importance of the Boston Harbor Islands in the nation's history.

The Harbor Islands are a place for renewal and reconnection. For centuries, the islands provided a rich and sustaining environment for human life. This disappeared in the twentieth century as wartime use for defense, pollution and waterfront development severed people's connection to the harbor. But with the cleanup of Boston Harbor at the end of the twentieth century, natural ecosystems have renewed themselves. The islands are being rediscovered as a setting for personal renewal and tranquility. As they were in the 1800s and early 1900s, the islands are once again a place to seek recreation and relaxation.

People perceive wilderness in many ways. To some people, wilderness is any wild, natural area. Others see wilderness as unknown and mysterious places. For still others, wilderness is connected in the imagination to our national parks.

The Federal Wilderness Act of 1964 defines wilderness as "an area where the earth and its community of life are untrammeled by man, where man himself is a visitor who does not remain."

By any definition, some of the Boston Harbor Islands are wilderness. However, none of the islands in the Boston Harbor Islands National Park Area was designated for inclusion in the National Wilderness system. (Although designation was considered for some of the islands during planning for the park.)

If we take the more general meaning of wilderness as a wild, unknown, mysterious place and add to this picture of the Boston Harbor Islands, like our western wildernesses, as alluring places that capture the imagination, then we can understand that, surprisingly, within the sight of downtown Boston lie these fascinating—and in many ways undiscovered—island wildernesses.

Perhaps the national significance of the park, its vital importance, is best illustrated by what E.O. Wilson, preeminent biological theorist and philosopher, wrote in 2005:

> *The Boston Harbor Islands are a natural laboratory seemingly made to order for research and education in biodiversity. They are small as islands go, yet highly variable in size, ecologically relatively simple, with a long history (for the New World) of European influence, and immediately accessible to a major urban center. These features combined offer multiple-opportunities for scientific discovery.*

What of the future of the Boston Harbor Islands National Park Area? It is a fledgling park, a unique model of management that has no track record. Its survival is not a foregone conclusion. Who knows, for example, what the effects of global warming will be on this maritime park in the twenty-first century? In any event, it will take the tireless efforts of people who are, in the face of shrinking government budgets for public parks and open spaces and self-serving politicians, bureaucrats and special interests, dedicated to preserving one of the nation's last urban wilderness areas.

Chapter 1

PREHISTORY

The Boston Harbor Islands were created eons ago when the crust of the earth shifted, setting off a cataclysmic upheaval of earthquakes, titanic floods and volcanoes, spitting fire and pouring forth molten lava. As the earth shook and rocked, a block of its crust broke off and sank, forming a lowland plain—Boston Basin. Millions of years passed and then the glaciers moved down from the north, grinding down ridges of land and leaving smooth, narrow hills of glacial till called drumlins. (In profile, drumlins look like upside-down teaspoons. The two most famous examples of these formations in Boston are Beacon Hill and Bunker Hill.)

As the glaciers melted, the sea rose in the basin and surrounded many of the drumlins. Some of these drumlins, such as Peddocks and Spectacle, became the islands of Boston Harbor. Other islands in the harbor, such as the Outer Brewster and Hangman's Island, are rocky outcroppings, formed as the ice sheet tore away pre-glacial soil and ground down the hills to bedrock. Still others—Governor's, Bird and Apple Islands —disappeared, obliterated in the modern era to make way for the expanded runway system of Logan International Airport.

THE FIRST INHABITANTS

During the Ice Age, sometime between twenty thousand and seventy thousand years ago, the ancestors of Native Americans or Indians crossed from Asia into North America over a frozen land bridge, now covered by the water of the Bering Strait. They entered a country that was bitterly cold and largely covered by glaciers. (In fact, scientists estimate that so much water was locked up in glacial ice that sea level was about three hundred feet lower than it is today, bringing coastlines close to the present edge of the continental shelf.) At the end of the Ice Age, as the glaciers melted away, these small groups of people moved into the newly exposed areas, close behind pioneer plants and animals. As yet, the Boston Harbor Islands were nonexistent. They were then, as one anonymous writer imagined it, "only barren, grassy hills standing above the broad wind swept coastal plain where mastodons and caribou grazed."

About twelve thousand years ago, Native Americans came to Massachusetts. Archaeological sites discovered on the Boston Harbor Islands in recent years provide the sources to establish a chronicle of the native use and their intimate knowledge

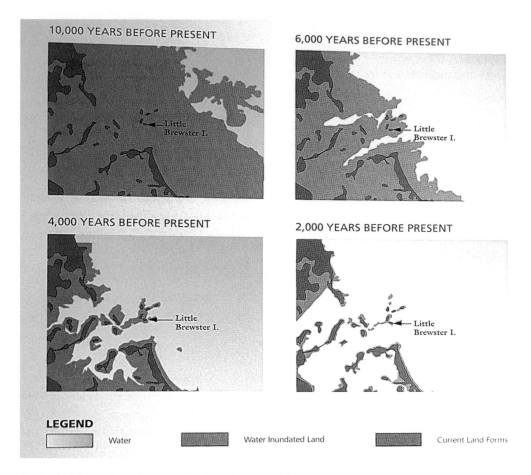

Geological formation of Boston Harbor. *Courtesy of the National Park Service (NPS).*

of the bounties of nature of the Harbor Islands. "Imagine yourself a Native visitor to the Boston area 8,000 to 10,000 years ago," Brona Simon, Massachusetts State Archaeologist, writes in *Highway to the Past: The Archeology of Boston's Big Dig*:

> *You would have come to here by dugout canoe or on foot. Standing on top of what is now Spectacle Island, if you looked to the east, you would see a broad coastal plain extending about eleven miles out to the ocean's edge. Dotting this forested plain would be hilltops that we now know as the Boston Harbor Islands and three major river valleys formed by what are now known as the Charles, Mystic, and Neponset rivers. As a hunter, you would see the advantage of the hilltops as lookouts for spying game. As a gatherer of wild plant foods, you would see the hilltops for their blueberries, hickory nuts, and acorns. As a fisherman, you would look to the rivers, ponds, and ocean.*

Move ahead in time to five thousand years ago. There are the same prominent hilltops from the past, but some of the outer hills are now islands and the seacoast is much closer, as the Ice Age glaciers continued to melt, enlarging the ocean and inundating the prehistoric coastal zone. In the Boston area, the former hilltops on the old coastal plain became surrounded by ocean water and became the islands of the harbor as we know today.

Between 3,000 and 1,500 years ago, the salt marshes and estuaries grew at the mouths of rivers and streams along the coast became, as Simon writes, "important locations for Native peoples to gather shellfish, hunt fowl, fish, collect reeds for basketry and obtain clay in order to make their own pottery."

Spectacle Island provides another revealing picture of Native American life between 1,400 and 1,000 years ago. In the 1660s, Spectacle Island was a ninety-seven-acre island located in the inner harbor just west of what is now Long Island. Spectacle got its name because to the early English settlers, it originally looked like a pair of spectacles. In 1992, archaeologists for the Central Artery Project (The Big Dig) excavated a shell heap or midden on Spectacle, containing thousands of clamshells. The site of the shell midden was adjacent to an ancient mudflat that was probably the source of the multitude of shellfish gathered by the natives.

Rare artifacts were discovered in the midden, artifacts discarded by the original native inhabitants, revealing significant information about their past activities. Discovered were bone points, awls and beads. Big Dig archeologists think the bone points would have been used for spear fishing and the awls for punching holes into skins for sewing clothing. Some arrowheads, knife blades, hammerstones and a decorative slate pendant were uncovered, as well as pottery shards and a tobacco-pipe bowl fragment. Food remains thrown into the midden included soft-shell clam, bones of codfish, small mammals and birds and hickory nut shells.

In the light of recent research, state historians and archaeologists, together, constructed an imaginary picture of life on Thompson Island one thousand years ago:

Exploring the islands. *Courtesy of* King's Handbook/*Friends of The Boston Harbor Islands (FBHI).*

On a summer day, a group of families arrive on the island. They settled at a beautiful, secluded area on the island with a small spring to one side, the sparkling blue ocean nearby, and tall oak and hickory trees overhead. Soft-shell clams were now the most abundant shellfish in the harbor and people collected them from a nearby clam bed and cooked them in clay pots, along with plant greens and the flesh of sturgeon and deer. Meanwhile, some of the families made stone tools, using stone from a wide variety of quarries including some so distant that the stone could only be acquired through trade. The children helped a little, but spent most of their time playing and splashing in the sun-warmed waters.

As the leaves began to turn red and gold in the fall, the families fished for cod, tautog, cusk, and other fish, and to hunt the cormorants, ducks, and migratory birds that flocked to the harbor at this time of year. Clams and hickory nuts were also collected, along with the last berries of the year. They gathered corn raised on the island in the summer and roasted venison to celebrate the harvest feast and enjoy the last of the good weather.

Off to one side, away from the cooking fires, some members of the group worked at making the stone tools they would be needing over winter, since good stone would be hard to find once snow was on the ground. In the evenings, everyone relaxed around the fires, some smoking their pipes and others dancing, wearing their best ornaments of bone and copper beads. Finally, one day, Indian Summer it is called in New England, the sky began to fill with clouds that signal an autumn storm, and the families quickly packed their belongings and left to go to their sheltered winter villages on the mainland.

Chapter 2

EUROPEAN DISCOVERY

Legend has it that in 1007 AD, while cruising off the coast, Norse Vikings from Greenland saw from their galleys the distant woody ridges of the islands of what is now Boston Harbor. Some accounts claim that the English explorers John and Sebastian Cabot, sailing down the North American coast in 1497, were the first to see them. Other accounts suggest that it was either Bartholomew Gosnold, an English voyager to this part of North America in 1602, or a Frenchman, the Sieur De Monts, in 1604 who first discovered the harbor's islands. Historical records show, however, it was Samuel Champlain, a French mapmaker and adventurer, who wrote the first description of the islands, sometime in 1605 or 1606:

> We saw numerous islands on one side and the other. We anchored near an island whence we observed many smokes along the shore and many savages running up to see us. All along the shore there is a great deal of land cleared up and planted with Indian corn. The country is very pleasant and agreeable and there is no lack of fine trees.

Champlain, however, left no map or precise description of the Harbor Islands. But Captain John Smith did. Smith, one of the founders of the Jamestown colony in Virginia in 1606, was exploring Chesapeake Bay and also the Potomac and Rappahannock rivers, when he was injured by exploding gunpowder in 1607. He returned to England and from that time devoted the rest of his life to promoting New England. (Smith originated the name "New England" for this region.) He made two voyages to the area in 1614 and 1615, and wrote, in a pamphlet, a description of New England, calling the area the "Countrie of Massachusetts, which is the Paradise of all these parts. For here are many isles all planted with corne, groves and berries, and salvage gardens. The land for the most part has high clayie, sandie cliffs," referring to Point Allerton on the Hull peninsula and Peddocks Island.

The Pilgrims depended on this tract and Smith's other books and maps when they sailed to the New World in 1620.

CITY UPON A HILL

As the three-masted *Arabella* sailed into Massachusetts Bay in 1630, John Winthrop and the ship's three hundred passengers, saw distant hills on the horizon. To their port side

The arrival of Governor Winthrop's fleet in Boston Harbor, 1630. *Courtesy of* King's Handbook/
FBHI.

were rugged, desolate islands now known as the Brewsters. As the *Arabella* sailed further
into the harbor, passing rocky outcroppings and hidden sandbars, they saw the islands
become more rounded and forested; these drumlin islands later were named Lovells,
Nix's Mate, Gallops, Long, Deer, Spectacle, Governor's and Noddles. The *Arabella*'s
destination: a settlement called Charles Town.

It was a year earlier, 1629, that Winthrop, worried about his declining law practice
in London and the future of the Puritans, was granted a charter from King Charles
I of England to establish a self-governing community in New England called the
Massachusetts Bay Colony. Unlike the Pilgrims who came to New England a decade
earlier, the Puritans were not separatists. They wanted to "purify" the Church of
England, not separate from it. When Winthrop concluded that reform was not possible,
he chose to make the long journey to the New World, as he said "to do more service to
the Lord." He said, "We have entered a covenant with God for this work. For we must
consider that we shall be as a city upon a hill, the eyes of all people are upon us."

When Winthrop and his followers reached Charles Town in 1630, because of the
scarcity of fresh water there, they moved across the river to "Blaxton's Peninsula," so
named for William Blaxton, the first English settler on this narrow, hilly peninsula.
(Also known as Shawmut Peninsula named after the Native American tribe that dwelled
there.) Blaxton, an Anglican clergyman with a taste for his own company, had settled
here in 1625, near an excellent spring on the western slope of what is now Beacon Hill.
The Puritans named "the city upon a hill" Boston, after the town in Lincolnshire from
where many of them came. As Boston's population swelled to 1,300, Blaxton, feeling

overwhelmed with his loss of privacy and solitude, left in disgust for Rhode Island in 1634. "I left England on account of the Bishops," he wrote, "I fear that I may have to leave here on account of the Bretheren." Blaxton's land was appropriated by Bostonians and turned into the Boston Common.

CASTLE ISLAND

Soon after the settlement of Boston, one of the first orders of business was to set up fortifications to defend the town against attack. As part of the governor's defense survey in 1632, an earthwork fortification was constructed on Corn Hill (renamed Fort Hill a few years later), an elevation inland from present-day Rowes Wharf on the Boston waterfront, commanding the heights over the inner harbor.

There was little danger of attack from the Native Americans, since the native population had been decimated by the plagues that swept through the tribes around 1616. The danger to the colony, the Puritan leaders believed, would come from the sea; not only from the French in Canada or the Dutch in New York, but from their fellow countrymen in England. The Puritans had come here to avoid subjection to the Church of England and King Charles I. The king was constantly arguing with Parliament over religious and political rights.

The issue came to a head when he suspended Parliament in 1629 and began ruling as an absolute monarch. The Massachusetts colony was afraid that King Charles would send out a governor who would support his majesty's established church and severely punish its opponents. The Puritan's fears were not groundless, for in the fall of 1634, a ship arrived in Boston with news that there were plans to compel the colony, by force if necessary, to receive a new governor and to accept the discipline of the Church of England. On their part, the colonists were determined to resist any attack by the king's navy.

Fort Hill, however, was of little value because its guns could not bombard and intercept enemy ships before they came within range of the town. Needing a defensive position, overlooking the main channel where enemy ships could be intercepted before they got into the inner harbor, the governor and his advisors sailed out to Castle Island, ascended its steep cliffs and decided it was the best defensive site in the harbor. Any vessel hoping to navigate the narrow channel into the inner harbor would have to sail head on for three miles within the range of the fort's cannons.

No one knows how Castle Island got its name. One local historian posited that sometime in the early years of the harbor's exploration, a ship was sailing into Boston Harbor and as it approached "this towering bluff of clay and yellowish gravel capped by a crown of trees," one of the crewmen exclaimed, "it looks like a Castle"—and so it was named.

Castle Island is a drumlin, a mass of sand, gravel, boulder and clay deposited by a melting glacier. The northern end of the island is high and was much higher in the seventeenth century than today, as erosion caused by the sea and northeasters have ground down the hill and deposited the soil on what is now the flat part of the island to the south. One writer at the time described it looking like "a shoulder of pork with the shank end southward." Consisting of about eighteen acres, the island was situated a mile and a half from Long Wharf in the town of Boston and about nine hundred yards from Dorchester Neck. (Castle Island is no longer an island. Over the years land fill has connected it to what is now South Boston.)

Upon the selection of Castle Island for Boston's major harbor defense, construction began immediately. The fort, completed in 1635, was comprised of dual wooden platforms linked by a wall of mud and masonry bonded by lime. Two cannons and a mud house constructed with crushed oyster shells were mounted on the platforms, prompting its commander to call it "a castle with mud walls."

Constructed out of these makeshift materials, it was not long before the fort collapsed and a new fort was built with pine trees, stone and earth. But the pine logs, exposed to the weather of Boston Harbor, were subject to rot and decay, so a third fort was built in 1653. This fort consisted of brick walls and contained three rooms: a dwelling room below, a lodging room over it and a gun room over that. In 1673, fire destroyed this fort, as the General Court biblically intoned, by "the Awful Hand of God." In its place, a four-bastioned stone fortification was erected.

Meanwhile, relations between the colony and the mother country were deteriorating. In 1684, the king revoked the Massachusetts Bay charter and sent a new governor, Sir Edmond Andros, to Boston. Andros had jurisdiction over the Dominion of New England, New York, New Jersey and Pennsylvania. No sooner had he arrived in town, Andros ordered the enforcement of the Navigation Acts, supported the Anglican Church's limits on the power of town meetings, questioned the validity of land titles around the harbor and, in short, established himself as a tyrannical ruler.

The Glorious Revolution in England (1688), in which William and Mary supplanted James II, provided the colonists with an opportunity to rid themselves of the odious Andros. When the news of the revolution reached Boston, the Puritan leaders seized control and imprisoned Andros in Fort Hill. But when Andros attempted to escape in a woman's apparel, as he passed the guards, he was discovered by his shoes; he had forgotten to change them. The authorities transferred him to Castle Island, a safer place of confinement. However, he escaped from there, too. Hoping to rally royalist supporters, he fled to Rhode Island, where he was captured and returned to the Castle. In 1690, the "whole Andros crowd" was shipped off to England. The king appointed a new royal governor and granted a new charter that made property ownership, rather than church membership, the qualification for voting.

FRENCH AND INDIAN WARS

King William's War (1689–1697) was the first of the four conflicts between England and France known in North America as the French and Indian Wars. The war was named after William of Orange, a Dutch prince who had agreed to become the English king in order to involve England in Holland's struggle with France. The war had alerted the colony to the danger from the French and was the compelling force behind the continued strengthening of the Castle. By 1697, the Castle's garrison had increased to 150 men and fortifications were built on Governor's Island, which lay across the harbor.

Castle William in the eighteenth century. *Courtesy of* King's Handbook/*FBHI*.

Although the war had ended, albeit inconclusively, the king was still concerned with the French in Canada. He wanted a stronger military defense against possible future French aggression. In 1698, he appointed the Earl of Bellomont, new governor of the Province of the Massachusetts Bay Colony—a domain that included New York, New Jersey, New Hampshire, as well as the command of the militias of Rhode Island and Connecticut. When Bellmont arrived in Boston, included in his entourage was Colonel Wolfgang William/Wilhelm Romer, chief military engineer to their majesties in North America, or as Romer liked to call himself "the architect for the Continent of America."

In keeping with the king's desires, Romer immediately began to survey the defenses of British territory on the continent. In January 1700, he issued his report dealing with all the fortifications from Hudson Bay and Newfoundland to South Carolina. The report stated that Castle Island was "of great security" to the town of Boston and should be repaired, expanded, maintained and paid for by the Province of Massachusetts Bay, since the colony was wealthy and enjoyed great privileges under the king.

To finance the fifth fort to be built, a tax was levied on all adult males, except the governor and his family; the president, fellows and students of Harvard College; ministers and elders of the church; schoolmasters and those too poor or disabled. There were also taxes on property; Native American, mulatto and black servants; oxen, cows, horses, swine and sheep; wine, brandy, rum, beer, ale, cider, perry—a fermented drink made from pears—mead and metheglin—a spiced version of mead.

Begun in 1703, Romer's "scientific fortification" was a four-bastioned brick fort armed with seventy-seven cannons, ranging from nine- to forty-two-pounders. The fort was surrounded by underground tunnels of "covered ways" for the movement of troops and gun crews. It was dedicated in 1703 and named Castle William, after William III of

Orange, King of England. Castle William's total cost: £6,645. On a flagpole standing eighty-five feet above the parade ground flew three flags: Great Britain's flag, symbol of British dominance in Boston; and the flags of the Massachusetts Bay Colony and North America.

Down through the years, Castle Island has evoked an aura of mystery, of strange and supernatural happenings. There were some in those times who believed the island was haunted, even cursed. Governor Winthrop recorded in 1643 "mysterious and unexplained lights" hovering over the fort. In 1665, lightning struck and killed the captain of the garrison as he stood on the ramparts. In 1673, a fire set apparently by the "Awful Hand of God" demolished the wooden third fort. During a gun salute marking the inaugural of the forth fort, a cannon exploded, killing two of the Castle's gunners. (Throughout its history, the Castle has been also used as a prison for royalists, Native Americans and Quakers, who were persecuted for their religion.)

Despite these bizarre events and tragic episodes, Castle Island continued to play an important role in Boston, Massachusetts, and the nation's defense for over three hundred years. Gerald Butler, a local military historian, wrote, "How carefully and prophetically the Puritan's choice of this site is borne out by the fact that Castle Island has remained an active defensive fortification from the seventeenth century through the Second World War."

Chapter 3

COLONIAL EXPANSION

Even before the settlement of Boston, there were European traders and settlers in Boston Harbor. Some years before the Pilgrims landed on Plymouth Rock, a French trading vessel was riding anchor off the shores of Peddocks Island, a 188-acre island lying across Hull Gut, a quarter of a mile from the Town of Hull. One night, Native Americans massacred all the white men on Peddocks, except five, whom they saved to exhibit before the various Massachusetts tribes. There is a story in the *King's Handbook of Boston Harbor* called "Peddocks Island and It's Tragedy" that tells what befell those Native Americans. It seems a Captain Dermer, who paid a ransom for the surviving French men, asked the Native Americans why they had killed the others. When they failed to give Captain Dermer a satisfactory answer, the captain cursed the Native Americans and swore that "God will destroy you for your bloody deeds." A short time later, so the story goes, smallpox savaged Peddocks Island. The "Red Men" died by the hundreds "in heaps and their carcasses lay unburied, left for crows, kites, and vermin to prey upon them." A visitor to Peddocks many years later described the piles of skulls and bones looking like the "field of Golgotha."

Among early settlers on the islands were David Thompson, who established a trading post in 1626 with Neponset Native Americans on Thompson Island, a 157-acre island lying off the Squantum section of Quincy; and William Noddles, who was the first settler on the island named after him in 1629. (Noddles is no longer an island; it became a part of East Boston in the nineteenth century.) Samuel Maverick was Noddles's first permanent settler. He erected a small, fortified mansion with artillery to defend the island and became the first New England slaveholder when he bought a ship filled with slaves from Tortuga in 1638 and sold them in Boston.

At one time, Noddles was heavily forested. But Native Americans of one of the Massachusetts tribes cleared acreage to plant corn, and later, colonists used the plentiful timber for fuel. As they cut trees, the colonists created pastures, and farmers began to ferry cattle from the mainland to graze on the island. During their years of suffering from persecution (between 1660–1670), the Baptists of Boston met on the island, away from the forbidding sway of the Puritan fathers, under the title of "the Church of Jesus Christ worshipping at Noddles Island in New England."

For his leadership in founding the Massachusetts Bay Colony, Governor Winthrop was awarded Conant's Island (soon after named Governor's Island), a green, hilly, seventy-two-acre island lying two miles from Long Wharf and less than a mile from Castle Island. (Governor's Island was leveled in the twentieth century and joined to East Boston as part of Logan International Airport.) The Governor's annual rent for the island was placed at a hogshead of wine and two bushels of apples. He planted, in what became known as the Governor's Garden, the first apple and pear trees in New England and "made gallant efforts to raise, also, grapes, plums, and other fruits." On the island, he built a large and comfortable main house to receive "royalty," a small dwelling for servants and a defensive blockhouse. Clearly, Winthrop enjoyed many happy days on his island, planting his garden and "regarding his rising metropolis across the channel with dignity and comfort," while "smoking his sweet and contemplative pipe" (and avoiding the Puritan law passed in 1637 banning smoking in public).

For a brief time, Governor's Garden was regarded as an island of demons by superstitious and witch-obsessed Bostonians. In 1648, the first of four witches was hanged on Boston Common. This was a prelude to the Salem witchcraft trials later in the century, which in the mass hysteria of that time held the belief in witches—individuals who had sold their souls to the devil in exchange for wealth or certain evil power over other persons. The devil aside, for the most part in these early colonial times, the islands' primary use was for agriculture or timber. One exception was Slate Island, where slate was quarried for houses and roofs, including King's Chapel in Boston. But on the other islands that were cultivable, cattle were raised, hay was harvested, fruits and vegetables planted and timber cut.

In 1634, the community of Dorchester acquired Thompson Island and for the next two and a half centuries leased it to several different families for farming. Bumpkin Island in Hingham Bay, just off the town of Hull, was bequeathed to Harvard College, which then leased it to tenant farmers for harvesting hay and growing fruits and vegetables. Cattle were raised on Rainsford and Nut Islands and trees were cut on Long and Deer Islands for timber and firewood in rapidly urbanizing Boston. But these islands that once offered such bountiful agricultural and natural resources for the Native Americans were no longer theirs. They were now owned by the white man.

Between 1630 and 1640, approximately twenty-six thousand English Puritans migrated to the Massachusetts Bay Colony in what was called The Great Migration. In the years between 1630 and 1633 alone, three thousand devout English men, women and children poured into the expanding settlements of Boston, Dorchester, Roxbury, Charlestown, Cambridge, Watertown and Medford. The burgeoning white population was now on a collision course with the Native Americans. Historian Howard S. Russell sets the backdrop for this clash of civilizations: "Assuming themselves superior and with an individually different concept of land tenure, the whites often dislodged him [the Native American] from his ancestral fields and his hunting grounds, bound him by laws in the making of which he had no part, and demanded his allegiance to a faraway king of whom he had never before heard."

The early explorers to the New World generally viewed the native inhabitants in a favorable light. Champlain called them handsome—"They are taller than Europeans." John Smith thought them "well-proportioned and goodly people." Bartholomew

Gosnold, among others, described them as "bronze or tawny, of gentle disposition and exceedingly courteous." But with the coming of the Puritans, it wasn't long before negative images began to creep into the perceptions of white settlers—images of "deceitful" and "immoral," conjuring up fear and antagonism. Steeped in the Old Testament and confident of their destiny as God's chosen people, the Puritans saw New England as an area God prepared for His elect. Whether soldiers, farmers, frontiersmen or clergymen, the white man's views were filled with prejudice. They had very little good to say about the natives. They saw them as thievish, lazy, improvident, licentious and downright bloody, murderous devils. Thundering from his pulpit, Boston minister Cotton Mather, whose sermons were later to incite the mass hysteria that led to the Salem witch trials, called them "wretches and blood thirsty savages...The most devoted vassals of the deval."

The Native Americans, however, did not have the power to fight against the white man's growing prejudice and encroachment of their land. The eastern Massachusetts tribes and the Wampanoag, Nipmucks and Pawtuckets were too weak to organize any formidable opposition. When increasing antagonism betokened war in 1633, a smallpox epidemic swept through the Native American villages of New England, decimating the tribes, along with any incipient rebellion. The disease, Governor Winthrop wrote in his diary, "cleared our title to their place."

Then in 1675, after years of enduring the colonists' growing power and arrogance and continued encroachment on their land, Metcom, the Wampanoag sachem, whom the English called King Philip, rallied the Naragansetts, Nipmucks and Pawtuckets to join him in a campaign to destroy the English and rid their homeland of these people. Led by Philip, the Native Americans went on a rampage of terror, attacking and burning colonial villages, laying waste over half of all the English settlements in New England. But as Harvard historian Jill Lepore wrote:

> *The Indians suffered far greater losses. Colonial armies pursued enemy Indians from Narragansett Bay to the Connecticut River Valley, killing warriors in the field and families in their homes...Always brutal and everywhere fierce, King Philip's War, as it came to be called, proved to be, in proportion to population, the bloodiest war in all of American history. And one of the most merciless: both the English and the Indians practiced torture, killed women and children, and mutilated the dead.*

Before the war was over the following year, there unfolded one of the darkest chapters in Boston's history. Just five months into King Philip's War, the Massachusetts Court ordered all Christian Indians imprisoned. Christian Indians were those Native Americans converted to Christianity by John Eliot, a zealous minister who translated the Bible into the Algonquin tongue, Massachusets, taught hundreds of Indians to read and write and established fourteen "praying towns"—Native American settlements built as Christian communities. (The first and largest was Natick, Massachusetts.)

Ironically, although these Christian Indian converts had lived among the English for years, the colonists didn't trust them. They feared these "praying Indians" would

Deer Island Treatment Plant—Deer Island. *Courtesy of the Massachusetts Water Resources Authority (MWRA).*

join Philip's campaign of terror. So on October 13, 1675, the Christian Indians were rounded up, marched in shackles through the countryside to the Charles River, placed on barges and transported to Deer Island—a bleak, windswept bit of rock situated in Boston Harbor, overlooking the main shipping channel from Boston Bay into the harbor. The two-hundred-acre island derived its name from the deer that fled from wolves on the mainland by swimming across Shirley Gut or crossing the ice in the winter. (Today, Deer Island is a peninsula, a part of the town of Winthrop and the site of the second largest wastewater-treatment plant in the country.)

Although estimates vary, it is believed that over a thousand Native Americans, both Christian and non-Christian, were interned on Deer Island, "an eerie foreshadowing of the fate of Japanese-Americans during World War II," wrote Lepore. "With little food and less shelter, probably half of the hundreds of Indians confined on Deer Island died of starvation or exposure during the relentless winter of 1675–1676." Many of those who survived fared little better, being taken off the island and sold as slaves in Barbados or Jamaica.

Native American internment on Deer Island was a tragic episode in American history. It marked a turning point in race relations between the Native American and English settlers. Not only did it strengthen and harden the enmity between the Native Americans and Anglos, the internment was instrumental in justifying Native American removals from the land. The conflict was the precursor to government policies, which institutionalized those governmental strategies and tactics used by the English in King Philip's War for the next 250 years. However, it would be just the first of many instances that Deer Island would serve as Boston's "Devil's Island"—a place of confinement for the city's "unwanted."

Today, Deer Island's legacy still haunts Boston. In the early 1990s, Native Americans protested the construction of the sewage treatment plant on Deer Island—the site of their sacred burial ground. A heated battle later raged between those who wanted to preserve Deer Island as a sacred Indian burial site, closed to the public, and those who wanted to include the island in the Boston Harbor Islands National Park Area. In June 2005, fearing the loss of a conference in the city because of an old law discriminating against people of color, after some 330 years, the Massachusetts Legislature finally expunged the act "Indians Prohibited Being in Boston" from the statutes.

Chapter 4

BOSTON LOOKS SEAWARD

When the early settlers arrived in the Massachusetts Bay Colony, they intended to become farmers. They quickly found out that New England's shallow soil filled with rocks and boulders, along with its long winters and short growing seasons, made it difficult to farm the land. It wasn't long, though, before they understood that it was the sea, the waters of Massachusetts Bay, that offered them sustenance—an abundance of fish, especially codfish.

Realizing they could trade fish for other staples with local Native Americans, the early colonists began to ship their fish to white settlements up and down the eastern seaboard. In 1631, an eighteen-ton vessel arrived in Boston Harbor, bringing corn and tobacco from farms in the Southern colonies; thus, trade routes were established between North and South.

Not only was the sea a source of wealth (the cod industry alone furnished a basis for prosperity), but good stands of timber from the northeastern forests encouraged shipbuilding and promoted trade. Oak timber for ships' hulls, tall pines for spars and masts and pitch for the seams of ships came from the region's forests. Concerned about their dependence on British trading ships, Boston, as the leading town in the Massachusetts Bay area, sought greater independence by starting a vigorous shipbuilding industry of its own, further strengthening the trade links with the other colonies and providing them with imports of English finished goods in exchange for exports of lumber and other commodities.

Building their own vessels and sailing them to ports all over the world, the shipmasters of Boston Bay laid the foundation for trade that was the envy of the other colonies and of their mother country. By the early 1700s, Boston's crowded shoreline, its forty wharves, numerous shipyards and six rope walks attested to its burgeoning maritime economy and thriving seaport. To accommodate the booming ship traffic, in 1716, the town erected Boston Light, a powerful beacon on Little Brewster Island at the harbor's entrance, to guide incoming ships. Boston Light, the oldest lighthouse in North America, played a strategic as well as a navigational role. Throughout the rest of the colonial period, Boston Light would raise the Union Jack to signal military authorities at Castle Island of approaching vessels. Castle Island would then alert the town to prepare its defense.

Boston Light on Little Brewster. *Courtesy of MWRA.*

Before the close of the colonial period, one third of all vessels under the British flag were built in Boston and other nearby towns along the Massachusetts coast. "By 1740, there were more than twenty shipyards working in the town," wrote historian William Fowler Jr.:

> *Boston could build ships at one-half of the costs of yards along the Thames. We were the Japan of the eighteenth century. The waterfront was studded with dozens of wharves, warehouses and shops. Sailmakers, coopers, riggers, teamsters and dozens of other trades owned their livelihood to the ships entering and leaving the harbor.*

Prospering Boston had become the busiest port, the hub of colonial commerce and the largest British town in North America. Boston's trade routes were trans-Atlantic: Europe, Africa and the West Indies, as well as to the other colonies. Imbued with their entrepreneurial vision, these so-called "codfish aristocrats;" these Yankee merchants— the Hancocks, Faneuils, Hutchinsons, Amorys—derived their fortunes from the sea, built their elegant mansions on Beacon Hill and instructed their captains "to try all ports." The commodities exported and imported included nearly every staple, domestic or foreign, that was current in the colonial world. Anything these Yankee merchants of the sea could get their hands on: fish, meats, vegetables, fruits, flour, Indian meal, oil, candles, soap, butter, cider, beer, cranberries, horses, sheep, cows, oxen, pipe-staves, boards, hoops, barrels, shingles, earthenware and woodenware, tobacco, sugar, salt, naval stores and wines, linen, crystal and furniture from England. Among the most profitable were molasses, rum and slaves.

THE SLAVE TRADE

Massachusetts was the first state to abolish slavery, yet it was also the first American colony to recognize slavery as a legal institution. Soon after Samuel Maverick of Noddles Island imported the first slaves from Tortuga in 1638, a number of Africans arrived in Boston aboard the *Desire*, the first authenticated American ship to engage in the Atlantic slave trade. In Boston, as in the rest of New England, slavery never took hold as an economic industry as it did in the southern states. Yet, Massachusetts merchants—and the growing Brahmin aristocracy that would eventually reside on the south slope of Beacon Hill—made their fortunes in the shipbuilding, rum and slave business. The Africans that began to arrive after 1638, principally from the British West Indies, became an integral part of the labor force needed to keep Boston's economy running.

They worked as distillers in the rum factories supported by the traffic in sugar from the Atlantic slave trade; they were the unskilled laborers in the port of Boston, where they served as stevedores, cargo handlers and dry-dock workers. Some of the Africans worked as skilled laborers, becoming printers, seamstresses, blacksmiths, carpenters and watchmakers. However, the actual number of Africans in Boston remained small. Less than 12 percent of the white population in Massachusetts owned slaves and the average number of slaves owned was between two and five. By 1700, there were fewer than five hundred Africans in the colony, with almost half of them living and working in Boston.

With the African population of New England numbering only about a thousand in 1700, Massachusetts was the largest slaveholding colony in the region. Yet, the status of Africans in colonial Boston was precarious at best. In 1641, the Massachusetts Body of Liberties became the first colonial court to officially sanction the institution of slavery. As late as 1670, Africans were still being referred to in colonial records as "servants" rather than "slaves." In that same year, the Massachusetts General Court ruled that the status of biracial children was to be determined by the race of their mother. Africans were also prevented from carrying weapons, selling their own liquor and intermarrying with whites. These laws and Boston's legacy of racial discrimination were to continue throughout the eighteenth and nineteenth centuries and well into the twentieth century.

One of the most enterprising, if unsavory, trading practices of the time was "the triangular trade." Boston merchants, as well as those from other American colonies, particularly in the North, developed the triangular trade to a large extent as a system of smuggling to evade British laws restricting colonial commerce and industry. Generally, the three points of the triangle were a port on the Atlantic coast, such as Boston, Newport or New York; a port on the Gold Coast of Africa; and a port in the West Indies, often Kingston, Jamaica. Vessels sailed from America carrying rum produced in colonial distilleries, cloth, trinkets and short iron bars that African natives used for currency. The goods were exchanged for slaves, gold dust, ivory and spices. The trip from Africa to the West Indies was known as the middle passage, on which many slaves died or fell ill. After selling the slaves, the ship captains purchased molasses, sugar, wines and other goods, usually from French traders, for the final leg of the voyage back to the American colonies.

A cache of eighteenth-century letters that was uncovered at the Medford Historical Society in Medford, Massachusetts, and reported by the *Boston Globe* on March 14, 1999, sheds some light into one local merchant's activities in the slave trade of Colonial America. While many Yankee merchants became fabulously wealthy as a result of triangular trade, the letters also reflect the grim price in human lives at the heart of many New England fortunes. The letters, written between 1759 and 1769, include instructions by a prosperous Medford merchant to a ship's captain on the treatment of slaves to be transported from West Africa for sale in the Americas.

The sailing orders penned by ship owner Timothy Fitch include lists on Africans based on height, advice on treating illness and avoiding mutiny among slaves and even tips on oiling the slaves' skin to ensure a proper sheen at auction time. In one of the documents, sailing orders issued from Boston in September 1761, Fitch writes to Peter Gwinn, captain of the brig *Phyllis*: "You are not to take any children and especially girls, if you can avoid it by any means and as few women as possible…but as many prime young men boys as you can get from 14 to 20 years of age…Take no slave on board that has the least defect," continues the ship owner's instructions. A bill of lading signed by shipmaster Gwinn aboard the *Phyllis* off the West African coast in May 1763 acknowledges receipt of "three men boys and three women girls burned on the right buttock with the bowl of a pipe," to be delivered "in like good order" to a merchant in St. Christopher's in the West Indies.

Merchandise listed aboard the *Phyllis* in an October 1762 voyage to Africa included 130 casks of rum, tobacco, sugar, axes, snuff, pitch, turpentine, musket balls, cannon shot and thirty-six bags of lobsters. An accounting record from August 1759 notes twenty-six slaves died during the voyage to the West Indies out of an initial cargo of "138 men boys women and girls and 1 child." In another letter, Fitch notes approvingly that Captain Day arrived in port with "70 or 80 of the primest slaves" whose good health made them sure to be "sold off immediately at a very high rate for cash down."

THE NAVIGATION ACTS

To force the colonies to trade exclusively with England and use only British ships, the British enacted a series of laws called the Navigation Acts. Beginning in 1651, a navigation act was passed restricting all trade within the empire to British, including colonial ships. The Navigation Act of 1660 listed specific colonial products as tobacco, cotton and sugar. The colonists could not sell these products to other European countries, where they might have gotten higher prices. In 1663, Parliament passed a navigation act that required the colonists to buy most of their manufactured goods from England. Furthermore, all European goods headed for the colonies had to be sent first to England, where the British unloaded the goods and collected an import duty on them. Then they reloaded the products on a British vessel and sent them across the Atlantic, thus protecting British manufacturers from the competition of their European rivals.

At first, the acts did in fact help protect America's infant economy by providing an outlet for its goods. However, as the colonies prospered, many colonists began to resent the trade restrictions. Some turned to smuggling; others turned to different ways to evade the laws of the high sea. In the seventeenth century, a time when European countries waged continual war against each other, privateers (shortened from "private men-of-war") sailed the seas with "letters of marque"—permission from a government to attack the enemy in wartime.

However, the line between privateering and piracy became blurred. Some privateers bent the rules and attacked ships of friendly nations, which constituted acts of piracy. Other privateers, even though they possessed licenses giving them permission to plunder enemy merchant ships, the enemy didn't necessarily agree with the legality of what they did. Spain, for one, viewed any such attacks on their ships as acts of piracy and treated captured privateers accordingly. With alliances shifting so frequently during the seventeenth century among warring Spain, England, France and Holland, a privateer could find itself attacking a former enemy ship before realizing that his country had signed a peace treaty with its former enemy.

Because of the English Parliament's unpopular trade laws that encouraged smuggling in cheaper goods on which no duties had been paid and no questions asked; because of the national rivalries in Europe for mastery of the seas and because of the strong temptation for treasure and vast riches, privateering gave rise to piracy. By the end of the seventeenth century, a pirate ship route was operating regularly out of New England. It was manned by a company of seamen, paid, outfitted and armed by wealthy merchants to sail the seven seas, plunder the ships of native traders and sail back to their home port with luxury goods to sell in the colonies.

Chapter 5

THE PIRATES OF BOSTON

B oston was home port for many pirates. Some were home-born like Joseph Bradish, who was born in Cambridge, Massachusetts, on November 28, 1672. Some were homebred, like Ned Low, who lived in Boston in 1719. And some were transient, like William Kidd, who took up residence in Boston for a brief time around 1696. Like New Englanders of today, the pirates wintered in the Caribbean. But unlike the latter-day snowbirds from the North, who travel to the Caribbean to relax in the sun, the pirates preyed on Spanish, Dutch, French and English ships laden with gold and silver from Central and South America, rum and sugar from Barbados and Jamaica, and wines, furniture and finery from Europe.

With the coming of spring, the pirates cruised north along the coast of the Carolinas, Virginia and up to New York, raiding coastal communities, capturing small vessels to obtain provisions and marauding larger craft bound with merchandise to and from England. As spring turned into summer, they proceeded around the tip of Long Island, then in a northerly direction again toward Martha's Vineyard, the Elizabeth Islands to Buzzard's Bay on Cape Cod. There they would wait with some certainty of capturing a vessel sailing through these waters. With their hulls stuffed with rich cargoes plundered in the Caribbean and booty stolen from vessels along the Atlantic Coast, the pirates headed for Boston, where they could fetch good prices for their contraband cargo.

The northerly route from Boston to Portsmouth, New Hampshire, to Halifax, Nova Scotia, was also favorite hunting grounds for pirates. Notorious pirates like William Kidd, Edward Teach, nicknamed Blackbeard, Samuel Bellamy and John Quelch roamed Boston's North Shore, known then as the "gold coast." And many of them are said to have buried their treasure on the Isles of Shoals—seven islands located about ten miles southeast of Portsmouth—and on the islands of Boston Harbor.

Captain John Avery, known as "Long Ben" Avery and one of the most infamous of the Madagascar pirates was said to have buried his gold and diamonds on two islands in Boston harbor. Edward Rowe Snow, the preeminent storyteller of the Boston Harbor Islands, said that when Long Ben Avery came to Boston he "buried his money at Point Shirley [then on Deer Island, now part of the Town of Winthrop] where it was later dug up. But his diamonds are yet to be found where Avery buried them—on Gallop's Island—centuries ago."

Nix's Mate in 1700. *Courtesy of* King's Handbook/ *FBHI.*

Nix's Mate—a channel marker today. *Courtesy of Ron Goodman.*

According to Robert Kidd, a descendent of William Kidd, Captain Kidd buried two chests on Conant's Island (renamed Governor's Island), containing from fifteen to twenty thousand pounds sterling in money, jewels and diamonds. Captain Kidd's treasure chests were said to be buried on the northeast corner of the island about four feet deep with a flat stone on them. A pile of stones was erected nearby as a marker. But over three hundred years, the tides and winds have radically altered the island; later it was leveled and joined with East Boston as part of the construction of Logan Airport in the twentieth century.

Kidd's treasure may still be out there. But who knows where? Is it buried under the runways of Logan? Or offshore, under the silt and sediment that now cover the harbor's bottom?

Boston was also the place where many pirates met their sorry end. The Stone Gaol, where pirates were held awaiting trial, was on the site of today's Boston School

Committee headquarters on Court Street. The place of execution is now the North End Park on Commercial Street. The Old North Meetinghouse, where Cotton Mather preached his execution eve sermon, was torn down for firewood by British troops in 1775.

There were two islands in the harbor where the bodies of executed pirates were left hanging in chains until they rotted away, as a warning to local seamen. One of them, Bird Island, was over time reduced to tidal flats and covered at high tide. It's now buried under the runways of Logan International Airport. The other island was Nix's Mate. Nix's Mate was at one time a sizable island where cows were known to graze Today, it is little more than a channel marker, dominated by a black-and-white shaped cement pyramid, as its shifting sands have washed away over the centuries.

No one knows how Nix's Mate got its name. One theory is that nearby Gallops Island was once owned by a man named Nix and the smaller island, also owned by Nix, came to be known as Nix's Mate. There is another explanation, though. Legend has it that a Captain Nix was killed at sea and that his mate was charged with the crime. When he was about to be executed on the island, Nix's mate protested his innocence and prophesied that the place that witnessed his judicial murder would be washed away by the angry sea.

> *Old Nix was a captain, hard and bold,*
> *And he reaped the sea, and gathered gold:*
> *He gathered gold, but one windy night,*
> *They found him dead 'neath the gunwhale light,*
> *And his mate stood near him, dumb and white.*
>
> *And his mate they seized, a young sailor he,*
> *And charged him with murder upon the sea.*
> *And brought him here where the island lay,*
> *Where the gibbet rose o'er the windy bay:*
> *'Twas more than a hundred years today.*
>
> *Here lay the ship, and the island there,*
> *And the sun on the summer oaks shone fair;*
> *And they took him there 'mid the chains to die,*
> *And he gazed on the green shore far and nigh,*
> *Then turned his face to the open sky,*
>
> *And he said, "Great Heaven, receive my prayer:*
> *The shores are green, and the isle is fair;*
> *To my guiltless life my witness be:*
> *Let the green isle die 'mid the sobbing sea,*
> *And the sailors see it, and pity me.*

"O Heaven! Just Heaven! My witness be:
Let the island beneath sink into the sea!

"Let it waste, let it waste in the moaning waves,
With its withered oaks and its pirates' graves,
Till it lie on the water's black and bare,
The ghost of an isle 'mid the islands fair,
Where bells shall toll, and beacons glare!"

He died, and the island shrank each year:
The green trees withered, the grass grew sere;
And the rock itself turned black and bare,
And lurid beacons rose in air,
And the bell-buoy rings forever there.

Source: *King's Handbook of Boston Harbor*

Bull Tavern was distinguished by a swinging sign in front displaying the beefy animal on either side. The tavern was found on the water's edge at the head of Bull's Wharf, which juts into Boston Harbor. With the addition of landfill into the harbor over the centuries, Bull's site today would be further inland, near South Station at an intersection of streets forming Dewey Square. Back in the "Golden Age of Piracy," roughly 1630 to 1730, Bull Tavern was a raucous place of merriment where seamen, waterfront denizens and pirates flocked to drink, carouse and tell tales of the high seas—tales of daring buccaneers who plundered merchant vessels for their cargoes of gold and silver, jewels, silks, sugar and furniture, and who smuggled these cargoes to merchants for great profits, tales of buried treasure and of hangings on the gibbet.

There is the tale of Thomas Pound, a Boston cartographer (renown in his time for mapping Boston Harbor), who in August 1689, set out with a crew from Bull Tavern to rescue Governor Edmund Andros. Andros had retreated to Castle Island and then fled to Rhode Island in the face of an insurrection that arose in Boston against his government's policies—a prelude of a greater revolution to come. But instead of heading in a southerly direction toward Rhode Island to rescue Andros, Pound set sail in an easterly direction until he was thirty miles southeast of the Brewsters. There he began his career as a pirate, capturing several ketches loaded with fish coming into Boston. He continued marauding up and down the east coast from Maine (then part of the Commonwealth of Massachusetts) to Cape Cod.

In September 1689, he was captured in the Elizabeth Islands off Cape Cod. Several days later Pound and his men were found guilty of felony, piracy and murder and sentenced "to be hanged by the neck until dead." The execution was set for January 27, 1690. Strangely enough, Pound's sentence was remitted. It was said that the influence of several prominent Boston merchants and particularly Governor Andros, who had survived the Boston insurrection, had much to do with Pound's escape from the gallows.

Captain Pound returned to England in 1699 where he lived as a country squire at Isleworth. Thus ends the story of Thomas Pound, who became a pirate and died a country gentleman—"a testament to the advantages of having friends in high places."

There is a tale of Ned Low, a Boston ship rigger, who went to sea with his brother in 1719. No sooner out of Boston Harbor, Low and his brother seized a small vessel, hoisted a black flag and embarked on a career of piracy. After capturing a Nantucket whaler, Low made her commander eat his own sliced-off ears, sprinkled with salt, before he killed him, acquiring the reputation even among his own men as a "maniac and a brute." For over a decade, Low sowed fear from Boston down the Atlantic coast, sailing as far as the Azores and East India. In a few months time, he was said to have captured nineteen ships in succession between the Leeward Islands and the Florida coast.

Low was finally captured in the Caribbean. After a quick trial, they hanged Ned Low on a specially erected gallows on Martinique. As he was about to be hanged on the gallows, a man standing in the crowd before the scaffold shouted "You monster!" Ned Low looked down coldly into the face of his own brother.

William Kidd was the most notorious pirate who ever sailed from Boston. Kidd started his career as a privateer in 1693. Kidd had been commissioned and financed with a newly refitted ship, the *Adventure Galley*, a 284-ton vessel equipped with thirty cannons by the Earl of Bellomont, Governor of the American colonies in the Northeast, the Lord Chancellor, the first Lord of the Admiralty, and other secretaries of state. Kidd's mission was the suppression of piracy along the American coast and elsewhere. The unstated purpose of particular interest to Lord Bellomont and his associates were the goods, merchandise and treasure taken from pirates.

But on a voyage to Madagascar, Kidd became a pirate, plundering ships of all kinds along India's Malabor coast. The holds of the *Adventure Galley* were already full when Kidd decided to plunder the *Qedagh Merchant*, a huge treasure ship of four hundred tons. After a brief struggle, the pirates boarded the ship and Captain Kidd was in possession of one of the greatest pirate treasure ever. Kidd headed for New York, believing all his plunder had been taken only from the French and other pirate ships. However, he was mistaken. Two of the ships and most of the booty he seized belonged to the Great Mogul, with whom Britain's East India Company desired to remain on friendly terms. Inviting Kidd back to Boston as a privateer in the King's Navy, Bellomont had sprung a trap.

Upon his return to Boston, Kidd was arrested, placed in the Stone Gaol and kept in irons. From Boston, Kidd, clapped in chains, was shipped to England where he was tried for piracy and sentenced to be hanged at Execution Dock in London on May 23, 1706. After sentencing had been pronounced, Captain Kidd said: "My Lord, it is a very hard sentence. For my part, I am innocent, only I have been sworn against by perjured persons." Indeed, he told the truth.

Kidd was hanged and his body dipped in tar, wrapped in chains and placed in an iron cage in the riverbed. For nearly twenty years, his body remained gibbeted along the Thames River to serve as a warning to all would-be pirates for years to come.

Chapter 6

THE "SPECKLED MONSTER" OF BOSTON

Smallpox was called the "speckled monster" in the eighteenth century. The disease appeared suddenly, like a minister of death, afflicting its victims with high fever, chills, swelling in the brain, back and muscle pain, prostration, nausea and vomiting. After two to four days, the fever relented and a rash appeared on the face and on the eyes. Then purplish skin lesions evolved into blisters and pussy pimples and finally dried into scabs that fell off after three or four weeks, leaving those who survived disfigured, and in many cases blind. The Europeans brought smallpox to the colonies, where it spread throughout Native Americans, nearly destroying them in epidemics of 1616—1617 and 1628.

Another smallpox epidemic struck the colonists in 1677, killing over a thousand people in the Massachusetts Bay Colony. It was at that time that town officials began to look at the islands of Boston Harbor, isolated and detached from the mainland, as a quarantine station for people from abroad. The town council ordered the passengers and crew of a ship infected with smallpox to spend eight days in quarantine on Deer Island before coming ashore in Boston. The fear was the infected ship could worsen the smallpox disease rampaging through the town. When smallpox epidemics broke out in Boston in 1690 and 1702, the town council decided to abandon Deer Island as a place to stop or send "sickly vessels" and chose Spectacle Island as a site for a quarantine center "both on account of the excellent anchoring ground and its remoteness from the town."

The most lethal smallpox outbreak occurred in Boston in 1721. Boston was a prosperous port town of eleven thousand residents when in April of that year, the British vessel *Seahorse* arrived in Boston Harbor from Barbados, bearing several passengers and crew who were infected with smallpox. Although Governor Samuel Shute ordered the ship quarantined at Spectacle Island, crewmembers had already come ashore and the infection spread. By early May, more seamen showed evidence of acute smallpox. Despite frantic efforts to quarantine the latest victims on Spectacle Island, cases were now appearing among the residents of Boston. On May 26, the Reverend Cotton Mather entered the following in his diary: "The grievance calamity of the smallpox has now entered the town…Because of the destroying angel over the town, a day of prayer is needed that we may prepare and meet our God."

About a thousand Bostonians immediately fled the community. Of those remaining, about six thousand were ultimately stricken with smallpox. Nearly 850 died of the

Port physician boarding inbound ship. *Courtesy of* King's Handbook/*FBHI.*

disease before the epidemic ran its course by the following year. Doctor Zabdiel Boylston (who, during the epidemic, introduced the technique of inoculation, which eventually lead to the eradication of the disease in the twentieth century) mourned the plight of Boston: "Parents being left childless, children without parents, and sometimes parents and children being both carried off, and many families broken up by the destruction the smallpox made."

Spectacle Island also served as a quarantine center in 1729 when town officials declared that all Irish vessels arriving in Boston Harbor were required to discharge their passengers and crew on the island, since ships coming from Ireland would likely to be carrying smallpox. Most passengers were transferred to the mainland, but many died and were buried on the island.

In 1736, the Massachusetts Court replaced Spectacle Island with Rainsford Island as a quarantine center. Rainsford, a small, eleven-acre island off of Long Island, was considered "a more convenient location, farther removed from the Town of Boston and with better 'roads' for safe anchorage of vessels." (Rainsford was later at times referred to as Quarantine Island or Hospital Island.) A year later occurred the first of several recorded instances of smallpox at Rainsford Island. Boston's selectmen met with His Majesty's Justices of the Peace, regarding information that "a Certain Negro Man was taken sick of the small pox at Rainsford Island, and that Several Persons dwelling on said island" were in danger of receiving and spreading the infection. The assembly agreed that the governor should be "acquainted with the Hazard the Town is in," so that legal measures might be taken to empower authorities to send sick persons to the island.

The very next day, Ebenezer Windborn was dispatched to the island as a guard "to hinder persons from Landing there, and also from going off said Island during the Continuance of the Small Pox there." The following year, the first official hospital to care for the sick that arrived by sea was opened. According to town papers in 1738, fearing the smallpox contagion, the province of Massachusetts Bay paid Constable John Harris for boat hire in carrying to the hospital at Rainsford "two men…lately arrived from Barbados…apprehended in danger of being infected with Small Pox."

Shortly after that, the schooner *Mermaid* put in at Rainsford, having sailed from Guinea on the west coast of Africa with John Robinson as shipmaster. Appearing before the board of selectmen, Captain Robinson declared under oath that he had come from the River Gambo "two and forty Days ago, with eleven White men on board and fifty slaves" and that they had smallpox onboard. While still 140 leagues up the river, he had buried three men who died, and "burnt brimstone to the vessel" to cleanse her. Subsequently, however, measles and the flux beset the schooner, fifteen slaves having died of the latter, two buried "in sight of Cape Cod."

The selectmen of Boston sent a committee that included a Doctor Rand and a Doctor Davis to board the vessel, wherein they found a hazardous stench and twelve of the slaves still sick. Finding it necessary "for the safety of the Town" that the schooner stay at Rainsford Island, provisions were made for the airing and care of the slaves who, according to Robinson, were "all young, under twenty years of age."

Throughout the rest of the eighteenth century, Rainsford Island was to be a way stop for the sick—and a final destination for the dead. In 1756, a sloop *Biddleford*, from Nova Scotia, with sick soldiers aboard, was given liberty to use the hospital at Rainsford Island for their accommodation. The following year, the schooner *Success* from Halifax was ordered to the island because of smallpox among the vessel's passengers, soldiers and officers. In 1777, during the Revolutionary War, Boston town clerk William Cooper ordered Captain Allen Hallet and the sloop *Republik*, arriving from the West Indies with smallpox aboard, to proceed to Rainsford Island and await further instructions. In 1793, the schooner *Neptune* arrived in Boston Harbor from Martinique with her captain dead of yellow fever and the first mate dangerously ill. It was recorded that "young doctor Rand is sent on board by Doctor Lloyd" and the vessel is ordered to proceed to Rainsford Island.

In 1793, a yellow fever epidemic sent patients from the town of Boston and from ships in Boston Harbor directly to quarantine on Rainsford Island. Yellow fever struck Boston again in 1799. The disease was believed to have stemmed from two young men who worked near the docks and then spread to the same neighborhood around Fanueil Hall. By many accounts, the symptoms of the disease included labored breathing, inflamed eyes, intolerable pain, a burning in the stomach, delirium, black vomit and death by about the fifth day. Unaware that the disease was mosquito-borne, Bostonians believed that the disease was caused by putrid fish, stagnant water, filth and offensive air. The only way to cope with the disease was quarantine. "Quarantine," observed one physician at the time, "has kept the Fever from spreading."

The keeper of Rainsford Island was instructed to police the island. If any person from a quarantined vessel attempted to bring packets or letters on shore, the keeper was expected to "forcibly detain him," all the while making certain crews from different vessels did not interact with one another. He was to insure that each person aboard ship would, for each of three days "wash his person with water and his hair with vinegar." The board of health consulted Boston's physicians as to the best methods of dealing with contagion and purification. Medical advice included the opening the cabin windows and doors on ships and diffusing the air with "Vapor of Nitre" and "Oil of Vitriol."

In 1832, the "Stone Hospital" (also known as the Greek Temple because of its architectural style) was built on the western head of Rainsford. Over the years, the hundreds of those who died from smallpox and other diseases were buried on the island. Before the tombstones were removed to Long Island some years ago, Edward Rowe Snow noted a number of their epitaphs. Two of these grim reminders of the mortality of man:

Nearby These Gray Rocks
Enclosed in a Box
Lies Hatter Cox
Who Died of Smallpox

Behold And See You Pass By
As You are now, So Once Was I
As I am now So You Must Be
Prepare For Death And Follow Me

Chapter 7

THE GATHERING STORM

For generations, England and France battled one another on the European continent, so it seemed inevitable that these two empires would clash for colonial dominance in North America. Over a span of seventy years, four colonial wars were fought between England and France—King William's War, Queen Anne's War, King George's War and the French and Indian War. The last and decisive conflict, the French and Indian War, gave its name to the whole series of these colonial wars. That final struggle pitted English colonists, who were confined to eastern seaboard settlements, against the French who blocked English expansion to the west and north. The British suffered a number of defeats in the first years of the war, but gradually, English naval, supply and numerical superiority turned the tide. The last French stronghold, Montreal, fell in 1760. Under the Peace of Paris, signed in 1763, France gave Britain all her North American holdings east of the Mississippi, except for New Orleans. From that time, France was virtually finished as a colonial power in North America.

Although the French and Indian War ended French influence in North America and greatly expanded British colonial claims on the continent, it also set off a chain reaction that led directly to the Revolution. The underlying question, the irresolvable issue between England and its colonies, was: Who would pay for the war—Great Britain or the colonies?

Taken in broad historical context, the overriding causes of the events leading to the Revolution had more to do with Britain's debts in financing an ever-expanding war in North America and that nation's determination to maintain its global commercial superiority than anything else. (A modern-day lesson for the American Republic?) Pitted against Britain's sovereignty was the American colonists' belief in their inherent rights to "life, liberty and the pursuit of happiness,"—and that meant the right to conduct their business and pursue their trade without any interference from the motherland. "No taxation without representation" became the colonists' political cry, but in fact, it was their economic pursuit that drove the separation between the colonies and the motherland.

Beginning in 1764, the English Parliament passed a number of acts over the next ten years designed to offset the war debt brought on by the French and Indian War. The Sugar Act increased the duties on imported sugar and other items, such as textiles, coffee, wines and indigo (dye). The Stamp Act placed taxes on such items as newspapers, licenses, almanacs, dice and playing cards. The Townshend Revenue Act taxed imports such as paper, tea, glass, lead and paints. Each act brought protests by the colonists, which in turn brought retaliation by the British as they would close the port of Boston and attempt to enforce the trade regulations.

In 1770, antagonism between British troops and citizens flared into violence in Boston when a mob pelted soldiers with snowballs and soldiers fired their muskets point blank into the crowd, killing three instantly, mortally wounding two others and injuring six. The incident was dubbed "The Boston Massacre" and the news spread throughout the colonies as an example of British heartlessness and tyranny. To calm down Boston citizenry, British troops were withdrawn from Boston to Castle Island, which became a Royalist headquarters from this point on.

Three years later, Parliament authorized the East India Tea Company to export half a million pounds of tea to the American colonies for the purpose of selling it without imposing upon the company the usual duties. Under the law, there was a three-penny-per-pound import tax on tea arriving in the colonies. East India Tea successfully lobbied Parliament to take this measure to save the company from bankruptcy. The effect was that the company could undersell any other tea available in the colonies, including smuggled tea. It also gave the company a virtual tea monopoly by allowing it to sell directly to colonial agents, bypassing any middlemen, and thereby underselling American merchants.

Boston merchants found this unacceptable. In November 1773, three ships bearing tea docked in Boston Harbor. On the night of December 16, 1773, the Boston Tea Party was held as the Sons of Liberty, an underground organization who viewed themselves as enforcers of the unofficial colonial government, disguised themselves as Mohawk Native Americans, boarded the ships and dumped all 342 containers of tea into the harbor. Parliament retaliated by revoking the charter of the Massachusetts Bay Colony and closed down the port of Boston.

Relations between England and the Massachusetts colony continued to deteriorate as Parliament passed the first of a series of Coercive Acts (called the Intolerable Acts by Americans) in response to what the Parliament saw as a rebellion in Massachusetts. The Boston Port Bill closed down all commercial shipping in Boston Harbor until Massachusetts paid the taxes owed on the tea dumped in the harbor and also reimbursed the East India Company for the loss of the tea. In response to the Boston Port Bill, Bostonians called a boycott of British imports.

General Thomas Gage, commander of all British military forces in the colonies, arrived in Boston and replaced Thomas Hutchinson as royal governor, putting Massachusetts under martial law. He was followed by four regiments of British troops, three of which were quartered on Castle Island. Tensions mounted further with another series of Coercive Acts, which virtually ended any self-rule by the colonies. Instead, the English Crown and the royal governor assumed political power formerly exercised by the colonists.

In September 1774, the First Continental Congress met in Philadelphia with fifty-six delegates, representing every colony except Georgia. Congress declared its opposition to the Coercive Acts, saying they were "not to be obeyed." A Declaration and Resolves was adopted that opposed the Coercive Acts and all other measures taken by the British that undermined self-rule and asserted the right of the colonists to "life, liberty and property."

In 1775, Parliament declared Massachusetts to be in a state of rebellion. Massachusetts Governor Gage was ordered to enforce the Coercive Acts and suppress "open rebellion" among the colonists by all necessary force. Gage ordered seven hundred soldiers to Concord to destroy the colonists' weapons depot there. At dawn on April 19, about seventy Massachusetts militiamen stood face to face with the British advanced guard on Lexington green. A "shot heard around the world" was fired and the Revolution began.

Chapter 8

THE MIRACLE OF DORCHESTER HEIGHTS

At the outbreak of hostilities, the islands of Boston Harbor continued to be used as they were in pre-Revolutionary times. British troops were quartered on Castle Island; and Castle William remained a refuge for Royalist sympathizers, fearing for their safety on the mainland. On Rainsford Island, during a smallpox outbreak in 1775, Dr. John Jeffries performed smallpox inoculations, injecting his own son, among other children sent to the hospital there. After the Battle of Lexington and Concord, a number of wounded Minutemen were taken to Rainsford.

Many of the islands were used as pastures for sheep and cattle and for growing hay. These islands became the sites of several brief, sometimes bloody battles (more often skirmishes) between the British and the colonials. The British needed hay for their horses and fresh meat to vary their salt-pork diet. The colonials needed the sheep and cattle to feed their growing army and at the same time deprive the British of the livestock and hay to literally starve them out of Boston. In the spring of 1775, shortly after the Battle of Lexington and Concord, continental soldiers crossed over to Deer Island where they took some eight hundred sheep and horses, captured a British barge and its crew and transported the valuable animals to American forces in Cambridge.

The following months saw more skirmishes. Continental soldiers raided Peddocks Island, carrying off sheep and cattle to the mainland and landed on Thompsons Island, burning a house, barn, orchards and crops. Under Major Benjamin Tupper, who became a favorite of George Washington, two hundred men in whale boats rowed from Dorchester to Governor's Island, captured twelve head of cattle and two "fine" horses, and returned safely without a loss. The continentals made a surprise attack on Long Island, capturing livestock and forcing the British to withdraw from the island. With the British gone, the continentals set up gun emplacements on the east head of the island, one of many early moves at securing American control of Boston Harbor.

The British, on their part, were not just sitting back on their heels. British soldiers landed on Lovells Island, seeking to buy some cattle for the sick at Castle Island. When the only two occupants of the island, two women, so the story goes, refused to sell, the cattle were taken with the promise that they would be paid for when the women presented the bill. Grape Island was owned by a prominent Tory of Hingham, Elisha Leavitt. He sent word for the British to come to the island to gather hay for their horses

quartered in Boston. When British soldiers arrived on the island, the alarm went out to the mainland. Soon, South Shore militiamen landed on the island and forced the redcoats back to their boats. "This glorified skirmish, which occurred on May 21, 1775," wrote Snow, "has gone down in history as the Battle of Grape Island."

Another encounter between British and Americans that could be more appropriately called a battle occurred in the summer of 1775. After a detachment of American troops burnt down the wooden parts of the tower of Boston Light on Lighthouse Island (later renamed Little Brewster Island), the British immediately began to repair this strategically important lighthouse. The Americans struck again. Once again under the command of Major Tupper, three hundred Americans attacked Lighthouse Island, killed several of the enemy and took twenty-three prisoners, with the loss of one American soldier.

Perhaps the most significant of all the fighting on the Boston Harbor Islands—the second land engagement after the Battle of Lexington and Concord and the first naval conflict of the Revolutionary War—was the Battle of Chelsea Creek, also known as the Battle of Noddles Island. After the Battle of Lexington and Concord, April 19, 1775, the British were driven back to Boston. The Patriots laid siege to Boston by completely surrounding the town on the land side, denying British General Thomas Gage access to hay, fresh provisions and other supplies. With the arrival of additional British troops to Boston, Gage needed more food and supplies for his troops.

Right: Courtesy of King's Handbook/*FBHI.*

Opposite: American militiamen. *Courtesy of Gerald Butler.*

To isolate Gage's army, the Massachusetts Committee of Safety advised that all animals and provisions be moved further inland beyond the reach of British foraging parties. To the east, the islands in Boston Harbor, however, offered much-needed livestock and hay. Noddles and Hog islands (no longer islands; both now part of East Boston) were comprised of a farm and pasture lands leased by Henry Williams. Williams had been running a profitable business, selling his livestock and hay to the British. The Patriots had no intentions of letting these islands remain a source of food and supplies for the British.

On May 27, 1775, Colonel John Stark of New Hampshire was ordered to go to Hog Island and remove all animals from the vicinity. Colonel Stark, with three hundred New Hampshire men, joined by volunteers from Chelsea and other towns of Massachusetts, crossed to Hog Island by fording a small, marshy creek that lay between the island and the mainland. The Americans removed over four hundred sheep and a number of horses and cows from Hog Island. Then, thirty volunteers crossed a marshy, knee-deep inlet that separated Hog from Noddles Island, known at that time as Crooked Creek.

On Noddles, the men made their way to the Williams farm, where they set fire to the home, two barns and the hay fields. Horses, cows and beef cattle were removed to Hog Island. What could not be moved was destroyed. As the Patriots were torching the Williams farm, they were met by a number of British marines, who were reinforced by four hundred

British regulars sent by General Gage. The British heavy fire forced the Patriots to retreat to a ditch in the marsh. Slowly, the British advanced in drawn-up lines until they were a few feet from the waiting Americans. The entrenched Patriots opened with a deadly fire, killing and wounding a large number of British and forcing them to retreat. Taking advantage of a break in the hostilities, the Americans withdrew across to Hog Island as British platoons fired across the creek at the fleeing Americans. From Hog Island, the Americans moved all the animals and themselves across the creek to Chelsea "neck."

Meanwhile, General Gage sent up Chelsea Creek the British schooner *Diana*, firing her six 4-pounders and twelve swivel guns, and eleven barges full of marines to cut off the American retreat from the island. With three hundred men and two cannons, commanding officer Israel Putnam of the Continental army came to the rescue of the colonial militia. In a fight that lasted all night, the Americans forced the crew of the schooner to abandoned her and flee, driving back the other vessels. They took the artillery from the captured vessel and beached and burned the British schooner (at the site today of the Meridian Street Bridge connecting Chelsea to East Boston). The fight was over. The colonials evacuated the livestock and burned Noddles, leaving a scorched earth for the British occupying Boston.

A ship of the King's navy was burned and destroyed in Chelsea Creek, under the nose of the British fleet. This was the first capture and destruction of an enemy war vessel by the Americans in war. The British command was disgusted with this affair. Lord Percy, the British commander in Boston, wrote home to his father: "The rebels have lately amused themselves with burning the houses on the island just under the admiral's nose; and a schooner, with four carriage-guns and some swivels, which he sent to drive them off, unfortunately got ashore and the rebels burned her."

General Gage, obsessing over the partial famine caused by the American raids on the islands, is said to have poetized:

> *Three weeks, ye gods! Nay, three long years it seems,*
> *Since roast beef I have touched, except in dreams.*
> *In sleep, choice dishes to my view repair:*
> *Waking, I gape, and champ the empty air.*

> *Come, let us plan some object, ere we sleep,*
> *And drink destruction to the rebel sheep.*
> *On neighboring isles uncounted cattle stray,*
> *Fat beeves and swine,—an ill-defended prey:*
> *These are fit visions for my noon-day dish.*

The Battle of Bunker Hill in June of 1775 was a stunning blow to the British high command in Boston. Although the British could claim the battle as a victory, it came at great cost in terms of men and material. Moreover, the battle marked a growing realization among the British command that this ragtag army of Massachusetts militiamen was determined to resist the overwhelming power of England. For both

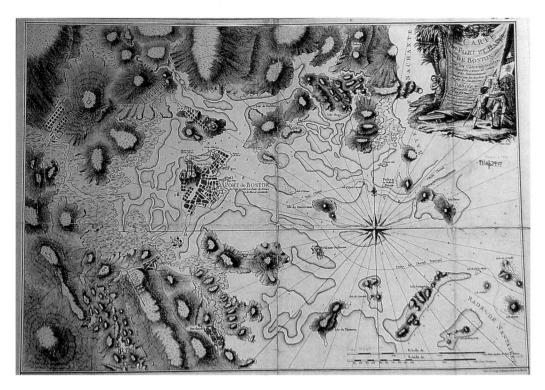

French map of Boston Harbor, 1775. *Courtesy of Levanthal Collection/Boston Public Library (BPL).*

British generals, Thomas Gage and his successor William Howe, the experience of Bunker Hill served to make both men more cautious and uncertain as to what course of action they should take.

In Revolutionary War times, Dorchester Heights was a "high, windblown no-man's land," comprised of twin hills at an elevation of 112 feet (nearly twice as high as Bunker Hill) on the Dorchester peninsula, overlooking Boston Neck, Castle Island and Boston Harbor. Both the Americans and British believed that whoever could command Dorchester Heights could control the fate of Boston. But, while both sides were aware of the strategic importance of the heights, says historian David McCullough in his book *1776*, neither side was daring enough to seize and fortify it. For the British command, their "immediate interest was the prospect of abandoning Boston, of packing up and sailing away," says McCullough. "Boston was clearly no place to launch an offensive operation. New York should be made the 'seat of war.'"

Some in the British command stated it more bluntly: burn Boston and move on to New York. Besides the strategic advantages of switching the offensive to New York, the British had other reasons for leaving Boston. For one thing, they hated the New England weather: The British could never get used to winter in Boston. Unlike the American troops, who were acclimated to the harsh winter winds and driving snows of the bay area, the king's men were unaccustomed to such a punishing environment. Moreover, the only lifeline for fuel and food for the town was the harbor and the open sea, but with the severe winter storms in the North Atlantic and the increasing number of American privateers operating offshore, fewer supply ships were getting through. These were miserable conditions for the British. Howe just wanted to get out of town.

George Washington had other plans. From the time Washington assumed command of the Continental army in Cambridge in July 1775, he wanted an all-out assault on the British. His generals cautioned against this strategy because it seemed too risky. Surround the town and wait, Washington's generals advised. Attacking the enemy where they were well fortified would court disaster. Instead, lure the enemy out as they did at Bunker Hill and then strike them. Washington finally concurred with his generals, and thus one of the most inspired and heroic actions of the Revolutionary War was set in motion.

The story of the Battle of Dorchester Heights begins in November 1775. Washington had the British bottled up in Boston, but he lacked the firepower to drive them out. Washington decided on a plan, one that was bold, original and utilized the element of surprise. Send Colonel Henry Knox, a twenty-five year old Boston bookseller turned artillery officer, to Fort Ticonderoga to fetch the cannons that Americans had captured from the British and now needed to combat the enemy in Boston. Knox had just become an artillery officer, despite having no formal experience. He learned about artillery from the books he sold as the owner of the London Bookstore (on what is today West Street, just off Washington Street in downtown Boston). The British officers would come in to buy books and Knox would ask them "How do you do this?" or "How do you do that?"

Aided by oxen, hired hands and farmers, Knox's men pulled and pushed sixty tons of artillery on sledges across frozen rivers, snow-covered fields and woods in a 250-mile trek from eastern New York to Boston. Iron cannons ranging from one hundred to fifty-five hundred pounds in weight, with some eleven feet long, were dragged 250 miles in winter on roads that were little more than rutted, poorly marked paths, up through the Berkshires, the men trudging with their feet wrapped in bloody rags because their boots had given out, leaving a trail of red on the white snow. When Knox and his men neared Boston, they faced a new challenge. How could they get the cannon to Dorchester Heights without tipping their hand to the British?

On the night of March 4, 1776, Knox and his men, joined by two thousand colonial militia and local volunteers and bolstered by four hundred oxen, crossed Dorchester Neck, a marshy area near present-day Andrew Square (in South Boston), that linked the peninsula of Dorchester Heights to Roxbury. They had to be silent because they were about 150 yards from the British positions on Boston Neck. To move in silence, they put hay on the road and wrapped straw around the wagon wheels to deaden the sound, pulled the cannon up the hill and entrenched them on Dorchester Heights. At daybreak, the British commanders looked up to the heights in disbelief. What they saw were the cannons of Fort Ticonderoga staring down at them ready to commence firing, prompting General Howe to exclaim: "My God! These fellows have done more work in one night than I could make my army do in three months."

The surprise was total; the plan worked. "As his pride and honor demanded," McCullough says, "Howe decided he had to attack now. He could not possibly accept the prospect of being outdone by the ragtag enemy, even if the carnage that had resulted from such an attack at Bunker Hill was as well known to him as to any man alive."

Howe gave the order for two thousand troops to assemble at Long Wharf and proceed by ship down the harbor to Castle Island, where an amphibious attack on Dorchester would be launched. Once again, as happened so many times in Boston's past, the hand of God seemed to prevail. As the troops pushed off from Long Wharf, "a storm raged with hail mixed with snow and sleet. The wind blew almost as a hurricane," wrote one diarist of the times, blowing the transports bound for Castle Island off course where they ended up across the harbor, grounded on Governor's Island.

General Howe had seen enough. He issued the order to evacuate Boston and sail to Halifax, Nova Scotia, Britain's major naval and supply center in North America. As one British officer wittingly expressed the mood of relief in leaving Boston: "Neither hell, hull, nor Halifax can afford worse shelter than Boston." On Sunday, March 17, 1776, the "largest fleet ever seen in America," wrote Abigail Adams in her diary, "upwards of one hundred and seventy sail" were in Boston Harbor, loading troops and royalist refugees. On board the ships were nearly nine thousand officers and men and over three thousand refugees. But only seventy-eight vessels sailed away on March 17; the others anchored further out in the harbor off Long Island. Before all the ships left, the British spiked their cannons on Castle Island and burned down Castle William; then they blew up Boston Light.

On June 13, American soldiers landed on Long Island and Nantasket Hill, from where they bombarded the remaining thirteen British warships still in the harbor, driving them out to sea.

The Siege of Boston, as this military operation became known, was a stunning success. McCullough describes Washington's performance as truly exceptional. "He had, indeed, bested Howe and his regulars, despite insufficient shelter, sickness, inexperienced officers, lack of discipline, clothing, and money."

Historian Joseph J. Ellis, in *His Excellency George Washington*, adds to this picture of Washington's debut as commander-in-chief:

> *Here for the first time we encountered the logistical challenge he would face during the ensuing years of the war. He met many of the men who could comprise his general staff for the duration. And here he demonstrated both the strategic instincts and the leadership skills that would sustain him, and sometimes lure him astray until the glorious end.*

Ellis raises another aspect of the Siege of Boston—the devastating effect of smallpox, "the speckled monster," and how it affected the outcome of the battle. (Smallpox and other epidemics occurred throughout the history of Boston, and their reoccurrence and the way the city coped with them played a major role in the history of the Boston Harbor Islands. During the American Revolution, a virulent smallpox epidemic of continental scope claimed about a hundred thousand lives.) According to Ellis, Washington first encountered the epidemic outside of Boston where he learned that between ten and thirty funerals were occurring each day because of the disease. Over 20 percent of

The British Blockade of Boston. *Courtesy of Massachusetts Historical Society.*

Washington's army at Cambridge was unfit for duty, the majority down with smallpox. He understood the ravaging implications of a smallpox epidemic within the congested conditions of his encampment, and he quarantined the patients in a hospital at Roxbury. Although many people opposed inoculation, believing that it actually spread the disease, Washington strongly supported it and began the policy of inoculation for troops serving in the Continental army.

"When historians debate Washington's most consequential decisions as commander-in-chief, always ongoing about specific battles," writes Ellis, "a compelling case can be made that his swift response to the smallpox epidemic and to a policy of inoculation was the most important strategic decision of his military career."

In the final analysis, though, given that the British had overwhelming military superiority, there is little debate among historians that the American victory at the Battle of Dorchester Heights was nothing short of a "miracle."

Even before the British departed, the Americans were strengthening their fortifications around the harbor, preparing for the day the British would return. Fortifications were constructed on Deer Island to guard the northern entrance to the harbor. A five-bastioned earthwork, designated Fort Independence, was built on Nantascot Head in Hull and garrisoned by militia from Hingham and adjacent towns to guard the southern entrance. Elsewhere, throughout the harbor, gun batteries and camp emplacements were built on Peddocks, Long, Lovells, Moon, Governor's and Noddles Islands. The fort on Castle Island was rebuilt and the American flag was hoisted above its parapets.

With France becoming an ally of America, the French built an earthworks fortification on Georges Island to protect their fleet in Boston Harbor. In July 1778, French ships, under the command of Admiral D'Estaing, sought refuge in Boston Harbor for his storm and damaged ships that had been driven from Newport, Rhode Island. Even though the British fleet, which was blockading the harbor, had a two-to-one superiority in ships over the French, the guns on the islands of Boston Harbor deterred the British from attacking. A few months later, Admiral D'Estaing's fleet sailed out of the harbor unmolested to the West Indies.

In August 1782, Bostonians rejoiced at the arrival of thirteen French ships. They had come to Boston to rendezvous with the French army under Rochambeau—the same army that had been with Washington when the British surrendered at Yorktown. When the fleet was moving up into the harbor, the *Magnifique*, a seventy-four-gun ship of the line, ran aground on the western end of Lovells Island. Badly damaged, the ship sank in the waters off the shore. The *Magnifique* was reputed to have been carrying a vast treasure of gold and silver coin. Edward Rowe Snow claimed that a few of these gold and silver coins were found in the nineteenth century. Perhaps, he suggested, there are more coins still buried in the sands off Lovells.

The French left Boston on Christmas Eve, 1782. Six weeks later, Great Britain signed the preliminary peace treaty. The Revolution was over. America had won its independence.

Although it is unlikely that the various battles and skirmishes on the Boston Harbor Islands altered the course of the Revolution, it would be fair to say that collectively the fighting that occurred there served to hasten British desire to get out of town and shift the war elsewhere. At the same time, the Battles of Chelsea Creek (Noddles Island), Grape Island, and, especially Dorchester Heights, like Lexington and Concord and Bunker Hill before them, served to rally Americans to arms, raise their morale and galvanize their determination—in the face of incredible odds—to keep on fighting for independence. During the Revolution, the islands were transformed from their primary use for agriculture to coastal protection and defense. The defense of Boston, the region and the nation became one of the major roles that the Boston Harbor Islands would play from this time forth.

Chapter 9

WAR AND PEACE

It was the year 1783. The war was over; the Treaty of Paris had brought peace. But Boston faced a severe depression because the war had disrupted its shipping industry, crippled its fishing and trading fleets and battered its coastal and overseas trade, as Britain refused to purchase American goods and effectively closed ports in the Caribbean to American trade. Bostonians discovered that they had won the war but lost their membership in the British Empire, as historian William Fowler Jr. called it, "the world's greatest and most prosperous Common Market."

To prosper once again, Boston would have to find new markets, new products and new trade routes. Boston also no longer had Britain to provide for its defense. The United States was buffeted by hostile empires bent in excluding the new nation from the profits of trade, and it was caught in the middle between France and England at war (1793) with her ships being seized by former friend and enemy. To strengthen itself against these hostile threats, the fledgling nation looked to build up its navy and forts along the eastern seaboard from Maine to Georgia.

In Boston, the first order of business was to rebuild Boston Light, which had been blown up by the British when they evacuated Boston. The new lighthouse, which had a seventy-five-foot tower added, was completed in 1783. Because of is strategic importance, the federal government took over Boston Light in 1789. Under the constitutional provision of providing for the common defense, the federal government assumed control of the other fortifications on the islands as well.

On Castle Island, the state prison and quarantine station operating on the island were shut down and construction began in 1801 to build a five-pointed bastion fortification consisting of forty-five cannon. The following year, construction was completed and the fort was christened Fort Independence by President John Adams. (This is the same fort that exists today.) To support Fort Independence, Congress recommended a fortification be built on Governor's Island across the inner harbor from Castle Island. Completed in 1808, the fort was an eight-pointed, earth-filled structure named Fort Warren, in honor of Doctor-General Joseph Warren, who was killed at Bunker Hill.

The War of 1812 was most unpopular in Boston. England and France had been at war since 1792. Looking to support their war effort with foodstuffs and materials, both sides intercepted American vessels and confiscated their cargoes. Any neutral ship

Above: Fort Independence, Castle Island. *Courtesy of Ron Goodman.*

Right: USS *Constitution. Courtesy of MWRA.*

trying to trade with one of the belligerents was subject to capture anywhere on the high seas. True, the war, in theory, was fought to redress the capture of neutral (American) ships and the impressment of American sailors; in reality, the merchants of Boston were reaping great profits in supplying both the British and the French with foodstuffs and materials. Although New England and Boston were thoroughly opposed to war, believing it would ruin their profitable trade with Great Britain, the south and west, eager for territorial expansion, clamored for war.

In June of 1812, President Madison, in response to British interference with American shipping during their blockade of Napoleonic Europe, proclaimed war with Great Britain. Despite the unpopularity of "Mr. Madison's War," all of the Boston Harbor fortifications were bolstered. A mix of federal troops and state militia known as *seafencibles*, were organized and sent to man the guns on the Harbor Islands' forts. Their task was to protect the harbor from British raids and provide a safe haven for ships running the British blockade.

At first, things were quiet along the New England coast. But Boston knew it would be just a matter of time before the British attacked the town, seeking revenge for their humiliating evacuation from the place where the Revolution had started over thirty years before. Sure enough, the British returned, but not to Boston; its defenses were too strong. Instead, they raided smaller, undefended ports, such as Plymouth, Kingston and Scituate, to get cattle, fruits and vegetables, often burning fishing boats in the harbors. Some towns on Cape Cod paid tribute to the British to avoid being torched. Truro, for one, paid the British $1,200 to spare it; Brewster, another Cape town, paid $4,000. But as far as Boston was concerned, the farthest the British penetrated was the Harbor Islands.

In July 1814, three British barges came up the harbor as far as Gallops Island and captured five sloops. But if Britain couldn't capture Boston, it could strangle it. By the end of 1814, the British had established a blockade between Cape Cod and Cape Ann. "Two frigates and several smaller craft patrolled Massachusetts Bay to keep American warships and privateers in port and to intercept any commercial vessels," wrote South Boston historian William J. Reid. American warships, however, couldn't be contained. They dauntlessly ran the blockades and boldly challenged the British on the high seas in what was to become a glorious chapter in the history of the United States Navy.

The USS *Constitution* ("Old Ironsides") was launched in Boston in 1797. When the war broke out, it sailed from the Potomac to its home port of Boston. From there, under Commodore Isaac Hull, she sailed by Fort Independence through the Narrows to meet and sink HMS *Guerriere* in a fierce duel fought in the choppy waters off the coast of Nova Scotia on August 19, 1812. The defeat of the *Guerriere* was the first major American sea victory of the war. In October, she put out to sea again with Commodore William Bainbridge in command. Sailing south, she came on HMS *Java* off the coast of Brazil and forced her to strike her colors. Avoiding the blockaders, she sailed to Boston but did not leave port again until December 1814. On this cruise, she captured the *Cyane* and *Levant* in February 1815, after the war was officially over.

Even in defeat the American navy achieved glory. On June 1, 1813, the British fifty-two-gun frigate HMS *Shannon* was patrolling Boston Harbor. While cruising several miles from Georges Island, the *Shannon*'s commander, Captain Philip Broke, sent a letter

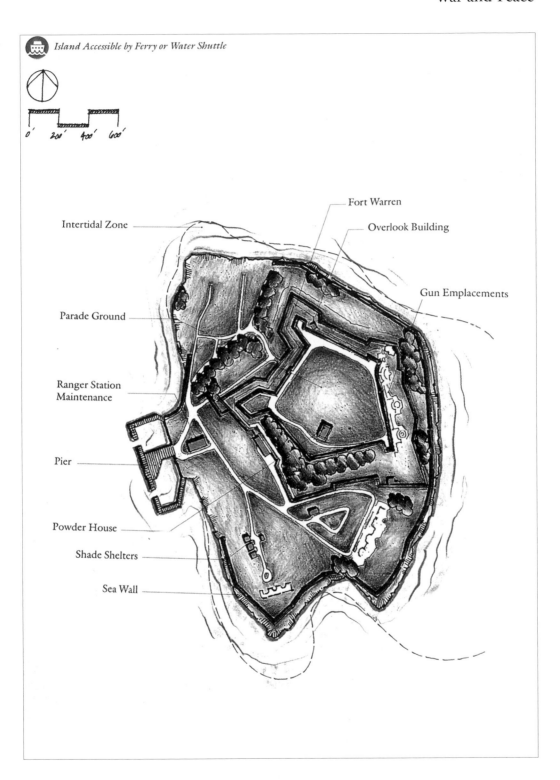

Island Accessible by Ferry or Water Shuttle

0'   200'   400'   600'

Intertidal Zone

Fort Warren

Overlook Building

Gun Emplacements

Parade Ground

Ranger Station
Maintenance

Pier

Powder House

Shade Shelters

Sea Wall

Fort Warren—Georges Island. *Courtesy of NPS.*

Interior of Fort Warren, view looking toward Hull. *Courtesy of Ron Goodman.*

to Captain James Lawrence of the forty-nine-gun American frigate USS *Chesapeake*, challenging him to a ship-to-ship battle. Taking up the challenge, the *Chesapeake* left her anchorage and sailed past Georges Island to engage the *Shannon* in a furious battle about twenty-one miles from Boston Light. When the two ships collided, British seamen swarmed off the deck, platforms and rigging of their ship and onto the *Chesapeake*, where the crews met in open combat. Both sides suffered heavy losses, but the British, fighting savagely and with great experience, were the victors. During the fierce battle aboard the *Chesapeake*, Captain Lawrence was mortally wounded. As he lay dying, he gave his final order, which became the rallying cry for the American navy: "Don't give up the ship!"

The Peace of Ghent, signed in December 1814, marked the end of the War of 1812. Nothing was said about neutral rights, blockade or impressments. Most of the burning questions that led to the war in the first place were set aside to be resolved at another time. Neither side received anything tangible in nearly three years of fighting. For Boston, though, what came out of the war was a feeling of pride and a growing sense of its importance for the new nation. In two years of fighting, many of the U.S. Navy's ships and the country's daring privateers came out of Boston and succeeded in doing what before then had seemed impossible: They wrested control of the shipping lanes from the powerful hands of the British by fighting the Royal Navy to a standoff.

Even more a source of pride and importance was that unlike Baltimore, Washington, and other towns and cities along the coast, Boston was never attacked or occupied. This was in large part due to the fortifications on Castle, Governor's, Noddles and the other islands of Boston Harbor. The prevailing naval thought—a theory proven successful by the unsuccessful British attack on Fort McHenry at Baltimore—at that time was that sailing vessels with the armament of the day could not successfully subdue land fortifications. The guns of Fort Independence, Fort Warren, Fort Strong and other harbor island forts protected Boston and deterred the British from attacking.

Certainly, fortifications on the Harbor Islands helped to deter any feared or anticipated attacks during the French and Indian War, the pre-Revolutionary period and the Revolution. It was in the War of 1812, however, that the Boston islands' fortifications, especially Fort Independence, established Boston as a citadel of defense, not only for itself, but for the new nation as well. Recognizing Boston's strategic importance, the Congress, in 1825, passed an act providing for "the preservation of the islands in Boston Harbor necessary to the security of that place."

Soon after, the federal government acquired Lovells and Georges Islands. Of the two islands, army engineers determined that Georges would make the best site for a fort. Georges Island had a commanding position overlooking the main shipping channel—the most strategic point, "right at the throat" of Boston harbor. No enemy ship could enter the inner harbor without passing directly by the island.

In 1833, the federal government appointed Colonel Sylvanus Thayer "the father of West Point," to oversee the construction of the fort. Two years later, construction began of the five-sided, pentagonal-shaped granite fort. It took over two decades to complete as each block of Quincy granite used to build the fort was cut and faced by hand, a process taking a single laborer two days to perform. The fort was named Fort Warren, (formerly the name of the fort on Governor's Island). Originally designed to hold three hundred cannon, the fort had ten-foot-thick granite walls, endless labyrinths of interior quarters for officers and enlisted men, a sweeping interior parade ground and massive parapets overlooking the harbor. It was considered one of the strongest coastal fortifications ever built in the United States. As one awestruck visitor wrote at the time, "the fortress surpassed even the Rock of Gibraltar."

Chapter 10

YANKEE TRADERS

It is the tale of puritans and pirates, of merchant princes and smugglers,
of opium, of clipper ships and packets.
—William M. Fowler Jr., *Boston Looks Seaward*

With the war over, Boston could once again concentrate its maritime energy on trade and commerce. Yankee traders resumed their dominance of coastal shipping. From Maine, Cape Ann, the North and South Shores, Cape Cod, New York, Philadelphia and Baltimore, small brigs, sloops and schooners carried timber, hay, potatoes, grain, lime, gypsum, soft coal, shingles, staves, bedposts, axe handles, grindstones, cattle, salt fish, cordwood and passengers to Boston. From the South and Deep South came tobacco, rice, cotton and naval stores. In return, Boston filled its coasters with shoes, boots, textiles and carriages—products manufactured in New England and imported products gotten from its China trade.

It was from the China trade that the Yankee traders, many of them from Boston and New England, built their fortunes. They sold porcelain, tea and silks at home in the United States—and smuggled opium from Turkey into China to pay for these desired goods. The who's who of nineteenth-century Boston Brahmins—Cabot, Bacon, Coolidge, Cushing, Forbes, Weld—all invested in the China trade. As Julian S. Cutler wrote in "The Old Clipper Days:"

When we sold the Heathen nations rum and opium rolls,
And the missionaries went along to save their sinful souls.

John Perkins Cushing (1787–1862) was a China trader and opium dealer, who served as an agent for respectable Boston families and firms from 1816 to 1831. He returned from China to Boston a millionaire, kept a grand house on Summer Street, complete with Chinese servants, and built a beautiful summer estate and gardens on top of a hill in what is now Belmont, Massachusetts. Cushing Square in that town is named for him. Cushing helped set up J&T.H. Perkins Company. The first Perkins cargo of Turkish opium, onboard the brigantine *Monkey*, arrived in China in 1816. When the transaction proved profitable, the firm dispatched an agent to Leghorn, Italy, to set up an opium-

Yankee traders off Boston Light. *Courtesy of the BPL.*

buying operation. It was the beginning of a thriving, if illicit, commerce for the house of Perkins.

In 1818, Perkins Company merged with Bryant & Sturgis, another Boston firm, to become what was called "the Boston Concern." The newly formed partnership held a virtual monopoly on Turkish imports to China. In 1829, the monopoly expanded as Russell & Company, a firm set up with the encouragement of Cushing and other prominent New England families, merged with the Boston Concern. By the mid-1830s, the opium trade had become "the largest commerce of its time in any single commodity, anywhere in the world." Opium smuggling didn't just make money. At times, opium was money. As one nineteenth-century historian remarked, "Smuggling was and is New England as a boiled dinner—and its history is at least as salty."

During the "golden age of sail" (1850–1854), Boston became the preeminent shipbuilding center in the country. The finest clipper ships were built in the shipyards of East Boston, also referred to as Noddles Island on nineteenth-century maps. The *Flying Cloud, Stag-Hound, Westward ho!, Romance of the Seas* and *Great Republic*, built by Donald McKay (his monument is located on Castle Island), were launched from the docks of East Boston. The Yankee Clippers—their sharp bows, sleek hulls and tall masts supporting eight hundred yards of white canvas—"cut their way through turbulent seas, which in bygone days never dreamt of such speed," as one nineteenth-century writer

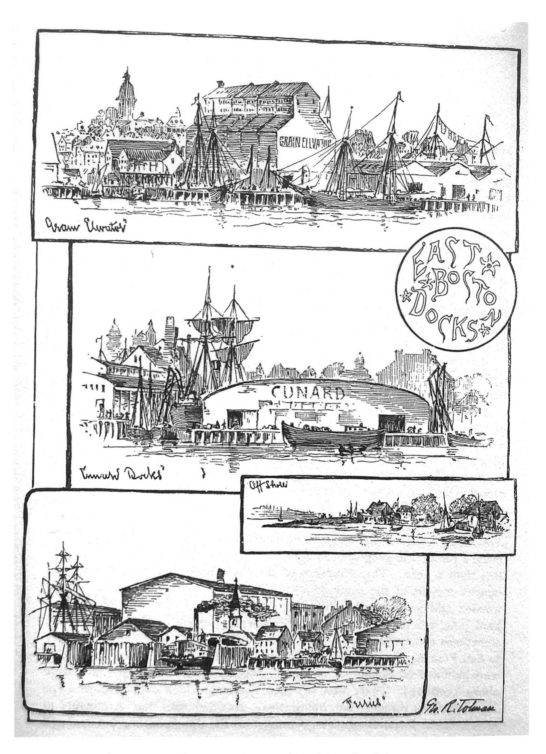

East Boston waterfront, nineteenth century. *Courtesy of* King's Handbook/*FBHI*.

observed. They "clipped" days off the sailing record of every journey they undertook—to Liverpool and Newcastle, to San Francisco, around Cape Horn to Hong Kong and Fuchow, China—and to the gold fields of California.

Boston historian Samuel Eliot Morison called the clipper ships "the noblest fleet of sailing vessels that man has ever seen or is likely to see," and wrote, in a classic passage:

> *A summer day with a sea-turn in the wind. The Great Banks fog, rolling in wave after wave…Out of the mist in Massachusetts Bay comes riding a clipper ship, with the effortless speed of an albatross…Boom-ending her studding sails and hauling a few points on the wind to shoot the Narrows, between Georges and Gallops and Lovells Islands, she pays off again through President Road, and comes booming up the stream, a sight so beautiful that even the lounging soldiers at the Castle, persistent baiters of passing crews, are dumb with wonder and admiration.*

Noddles Island was once an island separated from the mainland by Chelsea Creek and surrounding marshes (the site of the Revolutionary Battle of Noddles Island). Noddles disappeared a long time ago when it was transformed from an island into part of the mainland to open more land for commercial and residential development. In 1801, when Boston's population was twenty-five thousand, Noddles Island boasted but one mansion, a millpond dam and a wharf. Thirty-two years later, General William Sumner (the Sumner Tunnel is named after him) paid $80,000 for the island and founded the East Boston Company. The goal of the corporation, which owned East Boston, was to develop a trading center and a vacation resort. Landfill operations began at once. The East Boston Company graded the island by leveling its hills and dumping dirt into the surrounding marshes. Then it divided the land into four sections, fashioned streets in a grid pattern and sold house lots, creating one of the first planned communities in the city.

The company also saw the great potential for developing East Boston's waterfront. While commerce flourished in the 1830s, Boston lacked piers. So the East Boston Company built wharves, obtained a freight terminal of the Eastern Railroad and encouraged shipbuilders to locate their yards along East Boston's untapped waterfront. By 1835, 697 people were living in fifty private homes on the island; ten wharves lined the waterfront; and the Maverick Hotel, an elegant eighty-room resort hotel, opened that year. In the next twenty-five years the population exploded, spiraling from 1,400 to over 20,000 people.

No one is quite sure when Noddles's existence as an island actually ended. In 1882, M.F. Sweetser still referred to Noddles as an island in the *King's Handbook*. Suffice it to say that sometime during the latter half of the nineteenth century, through one landfill project or another, the geography of Noddles changed from island to mainland.

Chapter 11
NEW BOSTON

Following the War of 1812, Boston began a period of great expansion. Starting before the war, the town annexed South Boston (formerly Dorchester Neck and Heights) in 1804 and then pushed out in all directions. Land filling began in the Back Bay and the North and South Ends and Boston's boundaries expanded to include Charlestown, East Boston and Roxbury. (70 percent of Boston is built on landfill.) With its population swelling from thirty-four thousand in 1810 to forty-three thousand in 1822, the town of Boston was incorporated as a city that year. A year later, it was estimated at fifty-eight thousand. During this period, Boston transformed from a mercantile city to an industrial center. "The same money that financed the building of wharves and ships also funded the building of modern textile mills at river sites beyond Boston," wrote historian William Bunting. "These regional factories with their demand for thousands of mill hands, their need for large-scale supply of coal, cotton, wool and leather made Boston into a nest of portside warehouses and rail yards."

Along with the physical expansion of Boston came all the problems associated with urban life—poverty, disease, crime and congestion—and a strong humanitarian surge to solve these problems. Bostonians were fascinated in reform, especially reform directed to improving conditions for the poor, the imprisoned, the insane, the deaf and the blind. (The nation's first institute for the blind, the Society for the Blind, later the Perkins School for the Blind, was established in Boston in 1833.)

One of the influences of antebellum thought was that it favored isolation as the solution for social and public health problems. This made the islands of Boston Harbor a tempting location for facilities and institutions deemed unsightly and often seen as threats to the social order. Not only were victims of infectious disease, mental illness and poverty thought to be pernicious social problems that could undermine the social order, they were also believed to be more easily managed in the isolated setting of the Harbor Islands. This thinking led to the most intensive human use of the islands to house facilities that addressed serious issues of urban life. In short, the islands became the asylums for the city's social and economic outcasts—the homes of the unwashed and unwanted.

Similarly, this thinking led to the founding of the Boston Farm School Society in 1832 and the purchase of Thompson Island by the society for "the education of boys

Deer Island, nineteenth century. *Courtesy of MWRA.*

belonging to the city of Boston, who from extraordinary exposure to moral evil, require peculiar provision for the forming of their character, and for promoting and securing the usefulness and happiness of their lives; and who have not yet fallen into those crimes which require the interposition of the law to punish or restrain them."

Two years later, the Farm School merged with the Boston Asylum for Indigent Boys, which had been founded in 1814, in part, to care for boys orphaned by the War of 1812. The boys at the Farm School were taught the standard academic skills but also received training in farming and allied skills, such as carpentry. (The school was renamed Thompson Academy in 1956 when it became a preparatory school; farming ended entirely after the main barn burned down in 1963. Today, Thompson Island hosts Outward Bound and other youth programs.)

Deer Island was another favorite site for isolating the unwanted. As early as 1675, during King Philip's War, Native Americans were removed from their villages on the mainland and sent to Deer Island. Two years later, Deer Island was designated as a harbor quarantine station when passengers of an arriving ship were found to have smallpox and were housed there in temporary quarters. In 1821, Deer Island was considered for an almshouse because the old almshouse in South Boston was too small, overcrowded, in poor condition and generally not considered to "comport with the honor and interests of the Town." However, after inspecting the island, town officials rejected the site as having "poor soil, exposed location, difficult access and impracticality in winter."

Nearly three decades later, the city took possession of the island and established an Almshouse and a House of Industry there. These institutions were housed in a brick building completed in 1852. The Almshouse was established to serve the "virtuous" or "deserving poor"—individuals permitted to live on Deer Island when they were unable to support and care for themselves. Facilities provided for the Almshouse population included a nursery, schools, hospital, housing, workshops and a farm. According to the *King's Handbook of Boston Harbor*:

> *On the hill-slopes are the vegetable-gardens, abundant and successful; and here are raised enormous…beets, some of which weigh twenty-five or thirty pounds each…In the barns or on the hill are the gentle-eyed cattle; and, if one cares to see an endless number of pigs, an entire building is devoted to them on the southern point.*

The primarily adult inmates, including many incarcerated for drunkenness and idleness, of the House of Industry were sentenced by the courts to serve time at Deer Island for misdemeanors and crimes committed in the city of Boston. Although this criminal category of inmates was seen as a bad influence on the almshouse population, it was not until the construction of a reformatory and schools for pauper boys and girls during the latter half of the nineteenth century that a separation of the criminal and the poor was accomplished. In 1858, the House for the Employment and Reformation of Juvenile Offenders—Boys was located on the island for boys sentenced for misdemeanors such as truancy. A short time later, a House of Reformation—Girls was also established. The institutions for delinquent juveniles and paupers remained on the island until 1877.

Chapter 12

THE GREAT FAMINE

In 1845, a strange fungus attacked the potato crop—the mainstay of the Irish diet—in Ireland. By the fall of 1846, the fungus had ruined the country's entire potato crop. Starvation and disease stalked the land. For many Irishmen, the future looked hopeless. One possible goal to survive was immigration. By the tens of thousands, the Irish poured into America, landing at Boston and other East Coast ports in vessels called "famine ships," so-called because "famine fever," or typhus, broke out among the passengers on board the ships. Between 1846 and 1851, over a million Irish men, women and children left Ireland for North America.

In 1846, 65,500 Irish immigrants entered the port of Boston (compared to 3,600 from Great Britain, the next highest); in 1851, Irish immigration was nearly 64,000 (Great Britain was less than a thousand). During the six- to eight-week voyage, nearly 6 percent of the Irish who left on ships died at sea; 16 percent died either onboard or died shortly after docking. In the summer of 1847, the *Boston Transcript* reported the city was overrun with destitute, starving immigrants: "Groups of poor wretches were to be seen in every part of the city, resting their weary and emaciated limbs at the corners of the streets and in the doorways of both private and public houses."

Horrified by the hordes of immigrants and by their deplorable state, Boston authorities were infuriated, declaring the city a "cess pool of the civilized world." Moved by the prevalence of ship fever and by their humanitarian conscience, however, they passed an ordinance in the summer of 1847 to institute a quarantine station on Deer Island. All ships were obliged to submit to inspection by the port physicians; those with contagious sickness onboard were compelled to proceed to the south side of Deer Island and anchor there for a quarantine of twenty days, while the sick were transported to hospital sheds and tents. This measure, with the heavy penalties for bringing in fever-stricken passengers, achieved the desired effect: "sickly" ships avoided Boston, and Deer Island was never overcrowded.

The *John Clifford* was the first of many famine ships sent to quarantine. In the first week of operation alone, more than a hundred patients were sent to the Deer Island hospital. In the first six months at the hospital, 188 people died from typhus; another 70 died of complications related to the disease, such as dropsy, diarrhea and dysentery. The typhus fever, reported Dr. Henry Clark, one of the attending physicians on the island, "attacked its victims, suddenly causing chills followed by morbid heat of the skin, in many cases very

Irish immigrants landing on Deer Island, 1847. *Courtesy of MWRA.*

intense and pungent." It caused pains in the head, back and limbs; dizziness; stupor; deafness and ringing in the ears. It was, Clark explained, "a disease of debility; one characterization is the great indifference the patient manifests." (Typhus comes from the Greek word typhas, meaning "mist," a term coined in the eighteenth century to describe the clouded mental state of the patient.) Most of the 750 patients who died were buried in the Old Resthaven Cemetery located on the southern portion of the island. (In 1908, over four thousand bodies buried there over the years, including the Irish, were re-interred from the Old to the New Resthaven Cemetery, above the Hill Prison building, to make way for an expanded military reservation.) Several physicians died on the island while treating the immigrants' diseases, including Doctors Albert Upham and Joseph Moriarty, director of the hospital.

Between 1847 and 1849, over four thousand Irish immigrants passed through Deer Island quarantine station, many of them ill on arrival. On hand to care for them were several doctors and a dedicated nursing staff who saved thousands of Irish lives, provided physical comfort and solace to the dying and advanced the medical knowledge of famine fever to benefit of future generations. Clark and Upham kept careful notes and later published their findings in medical journals like the *Boston Medical and Surgical Journal* (forerunner to the *New England Journal of Medicine)*. Only about twelve cases of typhus were reported in Boston during this period. Nothing approaching an epidemic broke out and Boston authorities recorded that the city was saved "from a pestilence fatal to the health and business of the city" by the quarantine station at Deer Island.

In 1849, panic about an epidemic abated, and the quarantine station was closed down. Although the quarantine station was closed, the hospital continued to treat the Irish who were being shipped back to the island from Boston, where the unsanitary conditions of ghetto life afflicted the vulnerable just as the fever ships had. Some 160 men, women and children died and were buried on the island in 1850 alone. The names of the buried: Donahue, Finn, Cronin, Harrigan, Kelley, Gallagher, Donovan, Shanahan, McCann—the Irish roll call for the dead went on and on. Boston Irish historian Michael Quinlin called Deer Island, "a microcosm of the Irish Diaspora."

Although the Deer Island quarantine station stood as a glowing example of municipal reform, where the city accepted the responsibility to take care of its poor and sick, the division between the Boston Yankees and the Irish newcomers continued to grow more bitter. "The Irish, squeezed in their murky slums in their lowly occupations, and their dread of losing religion, never ceased to anticipate harsh treatment from strangers or to distrust unknown ways," wrote historian Oscar Handlin. "Continued struggles had engendered an acute weariness of Protestants, of Protestant friendships, and of Protestant assistance that often masked proselytization with the guise of benevolence."

The Irish associated poorhouses with all the disagreeable features of prisons in their native land. The horror of being exiled to such places prompted one parishioner to remark to his priest that "he would rather die on the streets than go to Deer Island." Despite their humanitarian impulses, Bostonians viewed these hordes of half-starved, disease-ridden, impoverished and unskilled Irish pouring into the city, in the words of one observer at the time as, "a massive lump in the community, undigested and undigestable."

By the 1850s, the Irish population of Boston had grown to 46,000, about one-third of the city's total population of 138,000. The growing power, at least in numbers, of the Irish made further clashes between Yankees and Irish inevitable. The white Anglo-Saxon Protestants detested the "vulgar" culture and religious practices of the Irish Catholics, calling them "shanty Irish." Above all, with the temperance movement now sweeping the country, the Puritan-minded Yankees detested the Irish immigrants' drinking habits—the grog shops, barrooms and saloons that popped up in South Boston, the Irish section of the city. In 1846, Boston had 850 licensed liquor dealers; in 1849, there were 1,200 dealers, most of whom were Irish.

With their population growing, the Irish began to demand a voice in politics and a vote in local elections. Fearing the Irish would take over local politics, nativists established an anti-Irish, anti-Catholic organization known as the American Party, or Know-Nothing Party in 1854. Members were called Know-Nothings because they claimed to be ignorant of the party's activities when questioned by outsiders. In truth, it was a party of hatred, intolerance and brutality.

The Know-Nothings spread their message of hate through the Yankee working class, provoking them into mobs of rage, egging them on to rampage through Irish neighborhoods, where they shouted racial slurs, beat up passersby, smashed windows and tore down crosses from the tops of Catholic churches. "They don't belong in this country! They shouldn't be taking jobs away from 'real' Americans! Go back to Ireland!" shouted the mobs. The fury in the streets eventually subsided; but the city was permanently divided and its character, politics and governance irretrievably altered. It would take the Civil War—which offered the Irish the opportunity to demonstrate their courage, valor and patriotism before the hatreds between the nativists and immigrants diminished and some mutual respect restored.

Chapter 13

THE CULTURAL HUB

Following the War of 1812, a great intellectual and literary stirring rippled across the land as America searched for a new national identity. Shedding their European influence, American writers began to describe the American landscape with an American voice. New England writers like Ralph Waldo Emerson, Henry Thoreau, Herman Melville and Nathaniel Hawthorne wrote about the wonder and natural beauty of the Berkshires, the Maine woods, and the Concord and Merrimack Rivers, but the Boston Harbor Islands did not escape their pen.

Richard Henry Dana, in his book *Two Years Before the Mast*, observed, sailing into Boston Harbor on his homeward voyage from California in 1836, Rainsford Island's "hospital buildings, nicely graveled walks and green plants." Emerson praised, "The three or four trees upon Apple Island make it a gem among the islands in Boston Harbor. What a scene would the Bay present, if all the islands were so covered!" Thoreau mused while sailing down the harbor "the isles rapidly wasting away, the sea nibbling voraciously at the continent…these wrecks of isles were being fancifully arranged into new shores as at Hog Island inside of Hull, where everything seemed to be lapsing into futurity…" (Thoreau would roll over in his grave if he saw the abomination of the once-bucolic Hog Island transmogrified into rabbit warren condominiums of today's Spinnacker Island.)

Author and travel writer Charles Dudley Warner extolled in the antebellum era: "What a beautiful harbor it is, everybody says, with its irregularly indented shores, and its islands!…The sky is cloudless, and the water sparkles like the top of a glass of champagne…Now we are busy running about from side to side to see the islands,— Governor's, Castle, Long, Deer, and the others. When, at length we find Fort Warren, it is not nearly so grim and gloomy as we had expected, and is rather a pleasure-place than a prison in appearance. We are conscious, however, of a patriotic emotion, as we pass its green turf and peeping guns."

Nathaniel Hawthorne once visited the Farm School on Thompson Island and his experience was reported in *The King's Handbook*:

> *A stroll round the island, examining the products, as wheat in sheaves on the stubble-field; oats somewhat blighted and spoiled; great pumpkins elsewhere; pastures; mowing ground—all cultivated by the boys…The farm boys remain insulated* [from the sailing

vessels], *looking at the passing show, within the sight of the city, yet having nothing to do with it; beholding their fellow-creatures, skimming by them in winged machines, and steamboats snorting and puffing through the waves. Methinks an island would be the most desirable of all landed property, for it seems like a little world by itself; and the water may answer for the atmosphere that surrounds planets. The boys swinging, two together, standing up, and almost causing the ropes and their bodies to stretch out horizontally. On our departure they ranged themselves on the rails of the fence, and being dressed in blue, looked not unlike a flock of pigeons.*

Castle Island offers the most famous literary setting for the Boston Harbor Islands. The story is told that back on Christmas Day in 1817, two officers fought a duel because one accused the other of cheating at cards the night before. A young lieutenant, Robert Massie, was killed in the duel by a lieutenant named Gustavus Drane, whom nobody liked. Massie's friends were angered at what happened and decided to avenge his death. They got Drane drunk, led him to a small compartment in the fort, chained him to the floor and scaled up the entrance. There is evidence that this incident really happened, for in 1905, some workmen who were renovating the fort knocked down the wall of the compartment and discovered a skeleton dressed in an old military uniform.

There was an enlisted man named Edgar Allan Perry in the Third Regiment of Artillery stationed at Castle Island in 1827. He later took the name Edgar Allan Poe and wrote a short story called *The Cask of Amontillado*. Poe changed the setting from Castle Island to Europe. It's a story of an Italian feud. The owner of a huge wine cellar wants revenge for the murder of one of his relatives. So he invited an unsuspecting friend, whom he thinks is the murderer, to join him in the cellar to sample the various wines. Lured in by the promise of better-tasting wines, the friend becomes more and more drunk. When they reach the depths of the cellar and the final cask—*The Cask of Amontillado*—the victim collapses in a stupor. The owner then bricks up the wall of the cask and leaves the man to die.

Chapter 14

TAMING THE WILDERNESS

The Puritan settlers arrived on the North American continent with an ancient bias. They viewed the New England wilderness as disordered and uncontrolled. They had a compulsion to transform the landscape that they encountered in the interest of survival. As the historian Roderick Nash observed: "The first white visitors regarded wilderness as a moral and physical wasteland, fit only for conquest and fortification in the name of progress, civilization, and Christianity."

Wilderness recreation was the last thing on the minds of men like John Winthrop, who saw the landscape as a wilderness to be tamed, and in what Winthrop praised as a "garden paradise," growing fruits and vegetables for their "city upon a hill." In the minds of the early settlers, safety and comfort, including the necessities of food and shelter, depended on overcoming the wild environment and transforming the wilderness into a productive garden.

At the same time, wrote Nash:

> *The indigenous people acquired significance as a dark and sinister symbol, and, consequently, the transformation of a wilderness into civilization took on the qualities of a morality play. In the colonial world view, morality and order stopped at the edge of the clearing; community and the controlling institutions of society served to check the "wilderness temptations" that imperiled the solitary individual in the New World—the American Indian.*

The Puritans objected to leisure activities for political as well as moral reasons. They were sharply critical of hunting and angling pastimes that were popular among the English aristocracy, and more importantly, of Indian males. As one Puritan apologist argued, the Native Americans were "not industrious, nor do they have art, science, skill, or facility to use either the land or the communities of it." Embedded in his assessment of Native American "leisure" and labor was both a moral judgment and justification for the expropriation of Native American lands.

While Calvinist tenets confined "sporting" to the streets of Boston, some residents disregarded these strictures. According to a Cultural Landscape Report on the Boston Harbor Islands, as early as 1677, Justice Samuel Sewall crossed the harbor "to Alderton's Point [Hull], and with our boat beyond…there catch'd fresh cod." In an early account of

Courtesy of King's Handbook/*FBHI.*

harbor recreation, Colonel Samuel Pierce confided to his diary that he "went frolicking in the water" in July 1765. Another reveler related, "gentlemen, sometimes in company with ladies spend the day partly on the water and partly on some of the islands in this very delightful harbor."

One of the first resort destinations in the harbor was Deer Island, where William Tewksbury operated a resort hotel, offering accommodations, a dance hall, lawn bowling courts and a beach from the 1780s until the mid-1800s. A popular legend of the day, which gave the island a certain aura of romance, has it that a headless ghost buried a thousand pounds of gold on the island.

The early decades of the nineteenth century witnessed the growth of leisure activities. Beginning in the 1820s, when Massachusetts industry turned inland, the harbor shores began to transition toward a landscape of pleasure. Pleasure parties sailed small boats to the islands and picnicked by the waterside. The first local resort and yachting center were established at Nahant, where summer villages were established in 1820 and open yacht races in 1845.

The popularity of the Boston Harbor Islands for recreational outings has been documented by the discovery of historical artifacts on the islands, including typical items of picnic debris, like fragmented ceramics and Kaolin pipes. These artifacts substantiate the comments of one nineteenth-century observer, who noted, "people encamped in tents, [during] the week after work, with small boats and yachts offshore, and camp kettles swinging gypsy-wise over their drift-wood fires."

Courtesy of King's Handbook/*FBHI.*

With the growth of an industrial economy and an emerging leisure class during the first half of the nineteenth century came a burgeoning tourist industry to northeastern United States. The grand hotel, situated in wilderness settings, served as an "early symbol of the economic and social flowering of the new Republic…a refuge for our well-to-do merchants…[and] a showcase for visitors," wrote John F. Sears, *Sacred Places: American Tourism Attractions in the Nineteenth Century.*

While the Boston Harbor Islands lacked the sublime setting that beckoned tourists to the mountains of New England, the islands attracted a diverse clientele. The Old Mansion House, built on the Great Head of Rainsford Island in 1819, hosted summer guests for many years. The island's nearby quarantine facilities also took in summer guests whenever no communicable diseases were reported on the island. On Gallops Island, following the death of her husband Peter in 1833, Margaret Newcomb established an inn and restaurant that became a popular summer resort. Excursionists came to Gallops not only to savor her famous clam chowder, but to search for the treasure of diamonds believed to be buried there by the pirate Long Ben Avery. Joseph Snow purchased the inn in 1855 and continued to run this thriving establishment until diminishing popularity forced the resort to close at the beginning of the Civil War.

For forty years, beginning in 1832, the Old Colony House attracted thousands of summer visitors to the Hingham peninsula, and it was the starting point for excursions to the nearby islands in Hingham Bay and to Cushing neck on World's End. The hotels in

Hull drew tourists to the pleasures of the harbor. The Pemberton, a large Queen Anne hotel at Windmill Point, had over a hundred rooms, a steamboat pier, a railway station and a grandstand for summer concerts. Its multi-leveled galleries looked out across Quincy Bay and Nantasket Roads toward the Brewster Islands.

In 1848, the Oregon House, another large hotel constructed with planks taken from the barracks at Fort Independence (later renamed Fort Revere) in Hull, opened to summer guests and autumn fishermen. Nearby on Peddocks Island, the white tents of camping parties occupied fields behind the Cleverly farm, which supplied fruits and vegetables to resort hotels on the Hull peninsula.

Spectacle, a 60-acre island with graceful bluffs set between Thompson and Long Islands in Dorchester Bay, was a longtime favorite destination for boaters and picnickers. As Spectacle's popularity with boating visitors increased, two entrepreneurs, Woodroffe and Reed, built two hotels on the island in 1847. Although these flourished as respectable resorts in their early years, they soon slipped into such illegal activities as gambling and prostitution. A police raid in 1857 to clean up the premises led to their bankruptcy shortly afterwards.

Long Island was the site for the most ambitious resort project. A group of speculators, known as the Long Island Company, started to purchase land for construction of a resort complex. From 1847 to 1866, main houses, cottages, wooden outbuildings and a three-storied hotel were constructed on the central part of the island. The seaside community, with its Long Island House and Long Island Hotel, was to be an elaborate planned recreational community in proximity to—yet completely different in density from—the city of Boston.

The Long Island Company realized their business venture was in trouble when it became clear that the island was no longer isolated from petty criminals and gangs. "The locality suffered from its proximity to certain unaesthetic quarters of the town,"

View of Boston Harbor from Fort Warren—Ballou's Pictorial, October 1857. *Courtesy of Metropolitan District Commission (MDC).*

wrote M.F. Sweetser in *The King's Handbook*, "whose adventurous young men found here a domain where the terror-inspiring helmets of the city-watch seldom intruded." Boxing matches, gambling, drug use and prostitution were among the unsanctioned recreational activities on the island. "Fishing picnics were replaced by Chinese picnics (opium parties). Romantic strolls on the island trails were replaced by police chases, and where men once cheered on racing boats they now cheered on the brutal beatings of their fellow citizens. These activities were well organized and well attended, and widespread among the islands."

The effort to create a seaside community on Long Island soon failed, and by 1882, after several changes in ownership, the location consisted of a few "shabby cottages." However, before the resort complex was doomed a failure, several of its outbuildings were used to house Union troops with the Long Island House on the Head serving as headquarters for Camp Wightman during the Civil War. A similar fate befell the other "pleasure islands" of Boston Harbor as the Civil War ended an era and returned the islands once again to their use for national defense.

Chapter 15
THE CIVIL WAR

Fort Warren has more memories of the Civil War days than any other place in New England.
                                                                    —Edward Rowe Snow

Following the attack on Fort Sumter (April 12, 1861), Massachusetts authorities were shocked to find the defenseless condition of the port of Boston. "In Fort Warren there was but one gun. In Fort Winthrop [Governor's Island], hardly twenty guns, and most of them were trained on the city itself. The casements were unfit for human occupation," reported the adjutant general of Massachusetts.

Nor were defenses any better on Castle Island. "Fort Independence has forty-three guns mounted, and is supplied with ammunitions, while only two men are there to defend it," reported the *Boston Post*. "A small privateer with a few men, might easily run in and take possession, destroy a large portion of the city and escape, all in one night," the paper told its readers.

Disturbed at the prospects of a surprise enemy raid, Governor John Andrew sent the New England Guards, also known as the Fourth Battalion Massachusetts Volunteer Militia, to garrison Fort Independence as an emergency measure. Under the command of Captain Thomas Stevenson, the Fourth Battalion was mostly made up of prominent Boston families, some of them still undergraduates at Harvard College. Among these Boston Brahmins were John Quincy Adams and Charles Francis Adams, the grandsons of John Quincy Adams, the sixth president, and the great-grandsons of John Adams, the second president of the United States.

In his autobiography, Charles Francis Adams wrote: "A pleasanter or more useful five weeks in the educational ways, I do not think I ever passed than during which I played soldier at Fort Independence in April and May 1861. I enjoyed the experience thoroughly, and what I learned there—the details of drill and of guard duty—proved afterwards of the greatest value to me." Elsewhere Private Charles Francis Adams referred to his experience at Fort Independence as a "military kindergarten."

When the Fourth was relieved of its garrison duty, most of the men joined other units; many of them commissioned as officers. Entering federal service in December 1861, the Fourth became the core of the Twenty-Fourth Regiment Massachusetts Volunteer Infantry, serving under Colonel Stevenson in the Burnside Expedition along the coast

THE BOSTON HARBOR ISLANDS

of the Carolinas, including Florida, the siege of Charleston and the siege of Petersburg. Stevenson later attained the rank of Brigadier General.

Charles Francis Adams received an appointment as first lieutenant in the First Massachusetts Cavalry. Despite his early remarks about his training at Castle Island, Adams served admirably in the Union army. He became a colonel in the Fifth Massachusetts Cavalry, a black unit, and led it at the occupation of Richmond. He also served at Antietam and Gettysburg. Later, looking back and comparing his experience at Harvard with that in the army, he wrote: "On the whole, I am inclined to think my three and a half years of military service and open-air life were educationally the greater value of the two."

As the war continued, men from all over the Northern states, as far west as Iowa, were recruited and sent to Fort Independence for training. These soldiers were formed into the Eleventh and Thirteenth Massachusetts Volunteer Infantry regiments, U.S. Army. Upon completion of their training, they were sent off to serve in the Army of the Potomac. The Eleventh fought at Gettysburg and sustained heavy losses at Spotsylvania. The Thirteenth's battle honors included Second Bull Run, Antietam, Fredericksburg, Chancellorsville, Gettysburg, the Wilderness, Spotsylvania, North Anna, Cold Harbor and Petersburg.

THE FIGHTING NINTH

When Fort Sumter fell, Governor John Andrew moved quickly to prepare the city for war. "He ordered the state militia to purge its ranks of those who would be unfit for the hardships of a military campaign," wrote William Reid. "With the approval of the legislature, he purchased military supplies such as overcoats, blankets, haversacks, and other military equipment." Most importantly, in terms of mobilizing the people for war, Andrew asked Thomas Cass, a Boston Irishman and former commander of the Columbian Artillery Irish Militia, to form the Ninth Regiment, the first all-Irish regiment.

In the spring of 1862, the unit, consisting of about a thousand Irishmen, boarded the *Nellie Baker* for a short trip to Camp Wightman on Long Island, where they began their training. Long Island has "green fields, pure salt air and a bright sky," wrote one soldier in his diary. "With pickets on sentry duty along the shore and tents pitched across the sprawling fields, Long Island looked like a true military encampment." Equipped with new 69-caliber muskets, the soldiers drilled and paraded under Cass's strict supervision.

In his book *Civil War Boston*, Thomas H. O'Connor said that "On Sundays, training was suspended and the men were allowed to roam freely about the island with family members and visitors who had brought food, refreshments and other items for their loved ones," and that Governor Andrew was pleased with the success in launching an all-Irish regiment. In ceremonies marking the departure of Irish troops to the war front, Governor Andrew thanked Colonel Cass for raising "this splendid regiment" and presented him with a flag bearing the Bay State emblem. "The United States knows no distinction between its native-born citizens and those born in other countries," said Andrew. Colonel Cass then unfurled his own regiment flag, made of green silk and inscribed on the front with gold scrolls: "Thy sons by adoption; they firm supporters and

Interior of Battery—Long Island Head. *Courtesy of* King's Handbook/*FBHI*.

defenders from duty, affection and choice." At the center of the flag were an American coat of arms, an eagle and a shield. On the reverse side was the Irish harp, surrounded by thirty-four stars and by a wreath of shamrocks. On June 26, 1861, the Ninth boarded three transport ships and headed out of Boston to war.

More than ten thousand Irish from Massachusetts fought in the Civil War, joining the Ninth, as well as the Twenty-eighth and Twenty-ninth, First and Third and Fifty-fifth regiments. More than two hundred men were killed in the Fighting Ninth, including Cass, who was mortally wounded at Malvern Hill in June, 1862. For the Irish, the war offered the opportunity to prove they were equal to native Bostonians. Their patriotism, their heroism on the battlefields and their pro-Union stand demonstrated they were first and foremost Americans.

The Irish contribution to the war brought a wave of tolerance throughout the city. Legislation was passed that stipulated that Catholic children would not be forced to read the Protestant version of the Bible in public schools. This piece of legislation, observed the *Boston Pilot*, the leading Irish newspaper in the city, "clearly acknowledges the loyalty being displayed by the adopted citizens in this hour of national trial."

The Irish also made another memorable contribution to the Civil War—a rousing marching song. Patrick Gilmore, a native of Galway, Ireland, was a Boston bandleader who composed a number of popular wartime anthems. In 1863, he composed his most famous anthem—"When Johnny Comes Marching Home." The song was "inspired by the ragged soldiers returning home from the front, on foot, by ambulance, or in coffins," wrote Quinlin. The song debuted at Tremont Temple on September 26, 1863, in a concert conducted by Gilmore. The tune, inspired by an Irish marching song called "Johnny We Hardly Knew Ye," was played by both Union and Confederate bands. The song became widely popular during the Spanish-American War in 1898 and has remained at the top of the list of America's patriotic songs. It was reputedly the favorite song of President John F. Kennedy.

> *When Johnny comes marching home again Hurrah! Hurrah!*
> *We'll give him a hearty welcome then Hurrah! Hurrah!*
> *The men will cheer and the boys will shout*
> *The ladies they will all turn out*
> *And we'll all feel gay*
> *When Johnny comes marching home.*

GLORY

The Fifty-fourth Massachusetts Regiment was organized in March, 1863, at Camp Meigs, Readville (now the Hyde Park section of Boston) by Robert Gould Shaw. Shaw was a twenty-six-year-old member of a prominent Boston abolitionist family and had earlier served in the Seventh New York National Guard and the Second Massachusetts Infantry. He was appointed colonel of the Fifty-fourth in February 1863 by Massachusetts Governor John Andrew. As one of the first black units organized in the northern states, the Fifty-fourth was the object of great interest and curiosity, and its performance would be considered an important indication of the blacks' commitment to the Union from throughout the North, particularly Massachusetts and Pennsylvania. Among its recruits were Lewis N. Douglass and Charles Douglass, sons of the famous ex-slave and abolitionist Frederick Douglass.

After a period of recruiting and training, the unit sailed from Boston Harbor and proceeded to the South, arriving at Hilton Head, South Carolina, in June of 1863. Soon after it saw its first action at James Island. The regiment earned its greatest fame on July 18, 1863, when it led the unsuccessful and controversial assault on the Confederate positions at Battery Wagner. In this disparate attack, the Fifty-fourth was placed in the vanguard and 281 men of the regiment became casualties (54 were killed or fatally wounded and another 48 were never accounted for). Shaw, the regiment's young colonel, died on the crest of the enemy parapet, shouting, "Forward, Fifty-fourth!" That heroic charge, coupled with Shaw's death, made the regiment a household name throughout the North, and helped spur black recruiting.

For the remainder of 1863, the unit participated in siege operations around Charleston, before boarding transports for Florida early in February 1864. Along with the Thirty-fifth United States Colored Troops, the Fifty-fourth entered the fighting late in the day at Olustee, Florida, and helped save the Union army from complete disaster. The Fifty-fourth marched into battle yelling, "Three cheers for Massachusetts and seven dollars a month," referring to the difference in pay between white and colored Union infantry, long a sore point with black troops. Congress had just passed a bill correcting this and giving black troops equal pay. However, word of the bill would not reach these troops until after the battle of Olustee, where the regiment lost eighty-six men.

After Olustee, the Fifty-fourth remained in the South fighting in a number of actions, including the battles of Honey Hill and Boykin's Mill before Charleston and Savannah.

The Fifty-fourth sailed back to Boston in August 1865, and on September 2, it mustered out at Gallops Island. (Earlier in the war, a training camp had been setup on Gallops Island. Long lines of wooden barracks were built, where at times three thousand recruits were quartered.) From Gallops, the Fifty-fourth was transported to mainland Boston.

Upon the unit's return, the *Boston Evening Transcript* published the following editorial:

> *The Fifty-fourth Massachusetts Regiment, the pioneer state colored regiment of this country, recruited at a time when great prejudices existed against enlisting any but so-called white men in the army, when a colored soldier was considered in the light of an experiment almost certain to fail, this command—which now returns crowned with laurels, and after two hundred thousand of their brethren from one end of the traitorous South to the other, have fought themselves into public esteem—had such a reception today as befitted an organization the history of which is admitted to form so conspicuous a part of the annals of the country.*

Nearly a century and a half after the war, the Fifty-fourth remains the most famous black regiment of the war, largely because of the popularity of the movie *Glory*, which recounts the story of the regiment prior to and including the attack on Battery Wagner.

FORT WARREN

At the outbreak of the Civil War, Fort Warren on Georges Island had only one cannon and when the first troops arrived, the fort was still not yet ready for occupancy. The Second Infantry Battalion (called the Tiger Battalion) from Boston arrived on April 29, 1861, and cleaned up the parade ground and living quarters. By June 1861, other regiments began arriving at Fort Warren. One of the first regiments training at the fort was the Twelfth Massachusetts (The Webster Regiment) commanded by Colonel Fletcher Webster—son of the famous statesman, Daniel Webster. The first guns to arrive were mounted on the ramparts facing Hull and the anchorage of Nantasket Roads.

"On October 7, 1861, the fort had 78 cannons mounted and emplacements ready for 54 of the new 10-inch Rodman cannon," according to Gerald Butler, former curator of Fort Warren. Daily life was harsh for the soldiers at Fort Warren, especially in the winter of 1861–1862. A Major Parker of the First Infantry Battalion wrote in his diary "such duty on a bleak island, exposed to the terrible cold and storms of a New England winter, was no pastime. Occasionally, some of the outposts would be untenable by reason of the dash of waves, and often inspection and relief of posts were effected with great difficulty because of the icy conditions of the ground."

Although living conditions were primitive, other aspects of a soldier's life on Georges Island were more pleasant. In his book *Fort Warren*, Jay Schmidt wrote that "rations for Union troops at Fort Warren consisted of fresh beef with potatoes three times a week, salt beef, pork or bacon three times a week and baked beans on Sunday." The soldiers' diet also consisted of tea or coffee and soft bread or hard tack each day. They entertained themselves by playing musical instruments, playing football, swimming in the ocean and

Union soldiers and lady, Fort Warren. *Courtesy of the Massachusetts Department of Conservation and Recreation (DCR) archives.*

Union soldiers loading cannon, Fort Warren. *Courtesy of DCR archives.*

catching fish and lobsters. The troops could also buy food from Boston cater
were allowed to visit the soldiers at the fort on Wednesday and Sunday. It is rep
on one day as many as two thousand people visited the fort.

In June 1861, the regiments training at Fort Warren began shipping off to war. The Eleventh Regiment shipped south and became one of the most frequently engaged Massachusetts regiments, fighting in battles from the First Bull Run to Petersburg. Shortly after, other regiments from the island shipped south, including the Twelfth, under Colonel Fletcher Webster. Webster was killed at Second Bull Run in August 1862.

Butler wrote that "while the Twelfth Regiment was quartered at Fort Warren, Private John Brown, a jovial young man of Scottish descent, endured a great deal of teasing about his abolitionist namesake's hanging in Virginia after the failed attack on the Harper's Ferry arsenal on October 16, 1859." Soon the regiment's glee club was singing, "John Brown's going to be a soldier" to the tune of a popular hymn, "Say Brothers, Will You Meet Us?" With the addition of other verses, the new song became "John Brown's Body." In July 1861, as the Twelfth Regiment paraded in Boston to receive their battle flags, the band struck up the new song and the men sang:

John Brown's body lies a-mouldering in the grave,
John Brown's body lies a-mouldering in the grave,
John Brown's body lies a-mouldering in the grave,
His soul goes marching on!

Glory, Glory, Hallelujah!
Glory, Glory, Hallelujah!
Glory, Glory, Hallelujah!
His soul goes marching on!

The song was picked up by other Massachusetts regiments and spread like wildfire throughout the Union army. When Mrs. Julia Ward Howe and Reverend James Freeman Clarke were visiting the Massachusetts Fourteenth Regiment on parade in Washington, D.C., they heard the men singing "John Brown's Body," the reverend challenged Mrs. Howe to create more meaningful words to the stirring tune. Thus, "The Battle Hymn of the Republic," the most famous Civil War song outside of "Dixie," was born. John Brown, however, did not survive the war. He fell off a boat and drowned while crossing the Shenandoah River near Front Royal, Virginia.

At the beginning of the war, Fort Warren's primary mission was to train Union recruits. By the fall of 1861, however, the federal government decided to use Fort Warren for Confederate prisoners. Overnight, six hundred prisoners were landed on the island, many of them suspected Confederate sympathizers from the border state of Maryland. As one of the prisoners described the fort on his debarking at the Georges Island pier, "a more desolate place could not be imagined this side of the Artic regions."

First impressions notwithstanding, in fact, captivity on the island was tempered by the people of Boston, who rose to the occasion and helped meet the needs of the new

View of Fort
Warren, *Harper's
Weekly*, 1861.
*Courtesy of DCR
archives.*

Guard House
and sentry box at
main entrance to
Fort Warren, circa
1865.

Garrison on Fort
Warren parade
ground, March
1864.
*Courtesy of United
States Army
Military History
Institute / Gerald
Butler.*

arrivals with gifts of food, beds and other supplies. Humane treatment of the prisoners was the policy of the fort commander, Justin E. Dimmick, a deeply religious old soldier admired by Northerners and Southerners alike.

Life for the prisoners varied, depending on status, rank and, of course, financial resources. While enlisted men from North Carolina had to cook their own rations in improvised pots, members of the Maryland legislature lived in high style. One of them, Lawrence Sangston, recorded in his diary:

> At half-past four, when we leave the parade ground and retire to our rooms, I trim and light my lamp, and prepare my writing table for those who wish to write, or read in quiet, leaving the front room for conversation, and the backgammon players...At ten o'clock, I brew a pitcher of hot whiskey punch, which we sip until eleven...Colonel Pegram gives us some very fine music from his guitar, and we put out the light and go to bed.

Hardly a life of deprivation and suffering! In fact, many Confederate officers and political prisoners were allowed to roam freely over Georges Island and to play football on the fort's parade grounds. Gifts and liquor from family and friends were also permitted, and there was even entertainment provided: fireworks displays on the Fourth of July and the Cadet Ball, where several young soldiers—dressed in borrowed finery—took the place of the absent ladies.

Yet, even the most comfortable of prisons is still a prison, and there were several escape attempts—all of them abortive—during this period of Fort Warren's history. Perhaps the most elaborate was the scheme devised by four Confederate officers who squeezed through a narrow musketry loophole in the fort. Two of them managed to swim across rough seas to Lovells Island, where they picked up a boat and sailed north, only to be captured by a U.S. revenue cutter off the coast of Maine.

Among the prisoners interned at Fort Warren during the Civil War years were George Proctor Kane, the police marshal and future mayor of Baltimore; General Richard S. Ewell, commander under Stonewall Jackson, captured at the Battle of Sayer's Creek and General Simon Bolivar Buckner, who had surrendered Fort Donelson to Ulysses S. Grant. When Buckner was ordered into solitary confinement at Georges Island, softhearted Commander Dimmick broke down and cried in sympathy. The result was that Buckner ended up consoling his jailer!

The greatest stir was caused by the arrival at Fort Warren of two Confederate commissioners—James Murray Mason, a former U.S. senator, and his colleague, John Slidell. The two men were sailing on the British steamer *Trent* to Europe, seeking aid for the Southern cause, when a Union warship, the *San Jacinto*, intercepted the emissaries and brought them to Georges Island. The event quickly boiled over into a *cause celebre*, and President Lincoln, fearful of an international incident, which would draw England into the war, arranged for Mason and Slidell's release. And so after a little more than a month's detention in quarters so luxurious that Union guards were grumbling and jealous, the illustrious commissioners sailed off from Georges Island.

Confederate prisoners of war at Fort Warren. *Courtesy of the DCR.*

Not only international, but national politics affected events at Fort Warren throughout the Civil War. For one thing, since Lincoln had suspended certain constitutional rights during the national crisis, including habeas corpus, alleged conspirators and Confederate sympathizers were arrested and imprisoned without benefit of trial. Thus, many of the political prisoners at Fort Warren were the objects of fierce moral and legal debates that raged throughout the country. Then, too, as Lincoln worked out complicated prisoner-of-war exchanges with the South, those who had been interned at Fort Warren would depart, sometimes as suddenly as they had arrived. One group of prisoners released in the spring of 1862 celebrated their last night on Georges Island with a farewell party that lasted through the night, dancing with the fort's laundry girls and drinking whiskey, which "flowed like water."

Not surprisingly, Boston politics played a role in the fort's administration. Conscious of the inhumane treatment of prisoners of war at such notorious places as Andersonville, Bostonians had tried hard to maintain Fort Warren's reputation for human decency. But during Boston Mayor Wightman's reelection campaign, the voices criticizing his leniency toward the Southern prisoners grew louder. Instead of sending homemade jellies to the prisoners, fumed the mayor's opponents, such officials "ought themselves be pounded to a jelly in the municipal election." Partly in response to this kind of feeling, the policy at Fort Warren tightened somewhat during the later war years; no gifts were allowed for a period, and troublemakers were summarily put in chains.

When the vice president of the Confederacy, Alexander Stephens—arrested at his Georgia home soon after the fall of Richmond—arrived at Georges Island one night in May 1865, he was first shorn of his money and papers, then confined alone in damp quarters in the cellar of the fort. Complaining of the damp and the poor rations

Arrest of Mason and Slidell at sea. *Courtesy of DCR.*

he received, Stephens wrote in his journal of "the horrors of imprisonment, close confinement, no one to see or talk to…Words utterly fail to express the soul's anguish. This day I wept bitterly." But a few months later, Stephens was released from solitary confinement and was allowed to wander about the fort as he pleased.

For other prisoners, with Lee's surrender at Appomattox and the general relaxation of tension that followed, life at Fort Warren had already begun to resume a more pleasant pace. Inmates were permitted to receive gifts once again, and there were also visits from Mary Salter, a young Boston belle who would sail by Georges Island waving her handkerchief at the prisoners, to which the Confederate inmates would enthusiastically respond with a Rebel yell. (Miss Salter, by the way, married Alexander Stephen's half-brother, Linton Stephens.) On October 14, 1865, Stephens and fellow political prisoner John Reagen, postmaster general of the Confederate states, were pardoned and released, departing the island on that afternoon boat. The last Confederate prisoners were released from Fort Warren in January 1866.

THE LADY IN BLACK

For many summers in the latter half of the twentieth century, the late historian Edward Rowe Snow was often seen with a large group of tourists in tow. As he led them through the winding passages and dark tunnels of Fort Warren, Snow would relate what has become the most popular ghost story of all the Boston Harbor Islands—"The Lady in Black." According to one version of this legend, a young Confederate naval officer named Samuel Lanier was captured and imprisoned in Fort Warren's "corridor of dungeons." In a daring rescue attempt, his bride of a few weeks disguised herself as a man and, packing a pistol, rowed across to Georges Island one stormy night. Although

Fort Warren—Georges Island. *Courtesy of* King's Handbook/*FBHI.*

she managed to rendezvous with her husband at the prison, the two were discovered trying to dig an escape tunnel. Desperate, the wife aimed her pistol at Commander Dimmick, but it exploded, killing her husband instead.

Our would-be heroine was sentenced to death as a spy, and chose for her hanging dress a robe made from the fort's mess-hall drapes. Ever since, so the story goes, the ghost of the Lady in Black has haunted Fort Warren, frightening away soldiers from their sentry duty during the long, lonely night. And apocryphal though the tale may be, as the wind howls through Fort Warren's mysterious corridors and turret staircases, echoing in its vaulted chambers and dungeon cells, all the ghosts of the Civil War still seem very much alive.

Chapter 16

TRANSFORMATION

After the Civil War, the Boston Harbor Islands resumed their pre-war uses. Most resorts reopened and new establishments welcomed an increasing number of vacationers. On Long Island, a second resort, Eutaw House, was constructed in 1873. Before the city of Boston acquired the property to house a municipal almshouse in 1882, "summer visitors enjoyed a pleasant view of the harbor from the hotel's long piazzas and from the rustling groves at the front of the property," wrote M.F. Sweetser in *The King's Handbook of Boston Harbor.*

Elsewhere in the harbor, in Hingham Bay, a footbridge was built in 1880 connecting a restaurant and observation tower on Ragged Island to the lavish summer resort at Downer's Landing, near Crow Point on the mainland. Other islands converted back to their pre-war uses as public institutions.

To make room for the expansion of public institutions on Deer Island, the quarantine hospital was moved to Gallops Island in 1867. Adding to the hospital facilities on Rainsford Island, military barracks were built to serve disabled veterans of the Civil War. In 1872, the city of Boston bought back the island from the state for forty thousand dollars and converted it into an almshouse.

From the beginning, there were complaints about the almshouse on Rainsford Island. Inmates, stating that they "are not criminals, " petitioned the city council of Boston to stop the "poor treatment," the dry bread and "bowls of slops" for breakfast and supper, and the water "unfit to drink." By the 1880s, there were some improvements of the treatment of paupers. These included "paid attendants for the sick and a visiting staff of physicians, preparation of food by an experienced cook" and "removal of insane patients to the proper asylums."

Pastime activities were introduced. A program for an afternoon's "entertainment" on the island, given on Washington's Birthday in 1886, lists vocalists, elocutionists, violinists, pianists and guitarists. A Summer Hospital for Infants and the House of Reformation for Boys were established on Rainsford in 1890. Although the infants' hospital operated for only three summers, it did give 250 mothers and children, most of them poor women with infants, the opportunity to receive medical care. The Boys House of Reformation held Boston's juvenile offenders, boys between eight and sixteen years old, as "inmates"

Scene on Ragged Island. *Courtesy of* King's Handbook/*FBHI*.

for offenses ranging from assault to playing ball on the Lord's Day, throwing a snowball or gambling in public.

In addition to military training, band practice and farming, the boys received vocational training in the island's own shoe, print and sewing shops. They turned out large quantities of shoes, mended and tailored garments by the thousands, produced meat from livestock, vegetables from the farm and printed their own magazine. In their spare time, they were treated to stereopticon lectures and banjo concerts on Sunday afternoons, skating in the winter, "daily baths in the ocean in the summer" and "rambles along the shore" to study plant and marine life.

The House of Reformation, however, had hidden stories to tell. After his discharge from the institution in the spring of 1898, one of the island's night watchmen, a man named Frederick Sanderson, told the press about child abuse on the island. A formal inquiry was conducted on "the allegations of the beating of children, depriving them of meals as a means of discipline, confining them in a dark closet as solitary confinement, and handcuffing troublesome boys to their beds at night, thereby endangering them in the event of fire." The inquiry resulted in the removal of the institution's superintendent and its athletic director, and the implementation of "general procedural reforms."

While the House of Reformation was replaced by the Suffolk School for Boys in 1906, the education of juvenile offenders continued to be a challenging task. There were serious arson fires and escape attempts, prompting the superintendent to report that many of the boys "never had a fair shot in life" and that the school should seek to "remold their characters and habits rather than get even with them for their failings." There were some improvements. The shoe shop was doubled in size, carpenter and cabinet shops were installed and a new cement piggery and hennery were nearly completed. Electric lights were also installed, and along with apple and pear trees, new shade trees were planted along the avenues, according to the Report on the History of Rainsford Island, prepared by the Institute of Maritime History, 2002.

By 1920, however, under the weight of increasing organizational and financial problems, the Suffolk School for Boys had to close its doors. "This past year was "a most trying one for boys and employees," according to the Annual Report of the City Department of Children's Institutions. "A fire of incendiary origins had destroyed a large wooden annex, containing lavatories, shower baths, toilets, recreation hall, tailor shop, and eight sleeping rooms." The report also described the institution's "terrible sanitary conditions," as student numbers increased to 179. Teachers and students were living without baths, except for a salvaged sink pulled from the ruins [of the fire], while toilets were placed in a schoolroom. Employees had to share not only rooms, but also beds. While requests were made for assistance and repairs, temporary measures would not address the overwhelming needs of the facility. The institutional era of Rainsford Island's history subsequently drew to a close.

Chapter 17

Prisons and Sewage Treatment Plants

After the Civil War, Deer Island was developed for multiple uses. The 1867 Annual Report on Boston's City Institutions noted that the close association of pauper children with pauper men in the almshouse had a bad effect on the children. The solution to the problem was to renovate and convert a former dairy building to house the boys separately. Then a new brick building was constructed to house the girls.

Because of the overcrowded conditions on the mainland, a house of correction was established on Deer Island in 1882. Some inmates from the house of correction in Boston were sent to Concord Reformatory; the rest went to Deer Island. Deer Island's house of correction was not considered a reformatory, but "merely a place of punishment and detention." Men were employed in many occupations on the island, including farming, stone cutting, and manufacturing a number of items. By 1896, however, the institution formerly known as the House of Industry on Deer Island was established as the Suffolk County House of Correction at Deer Island. The first prison building on the island, New Prison, housed inmates until it was razed in the 1960s. In 1902, the last of the inmates housed in the House of Correction in South Boston were moved to Deer Island's House of Correction, the only city of Boston institution still located on the island. All other residents in the almshouse and schools had been moved to other locations.

A second structure, built in 1902 and known as Hill Prison, increased the total population on the island to nearly a thousand. For its time, Hill Prison was a model facility with classrooms, shops and a dining hall. The prison was demolished in 1991 to make way for a new primary and secondary wastewater-treatment plant. The inmates were relocated to a newer facility in South Boston, thus ending one of the oldest continuing penal institutions in the Western hemisphere.

Meanwhile in Boston, there was growing concern and alarm about the city's sewage situation. A cholera outbreak in 1865 started a hue and cry for better sewage management. Citing deplorable sanitary conditions in Boston, municipal physicians urged the city to improve the sewerage system "as soon as possible." In 1875, the mayor of Boston appointed a commission to report on the city's sewerage system and to recommend ways to upgrade it. The commission proposed that two main drainage systems be built, one for the area north and one for the area south of the Charles River. Sewage treatment called for a steam-driven pumping station to be built on Deer Island.

By 1900, the North Metropolitan Sewerage System, serving fourteen cities and towns, was fully operational.

The pumping station at Deer Island was the largest of three stations constructed to pump sewage through the system. Wastewater was sent to the island and screened to remove large objects, then pumped without any treatment into Boston Harbor. At the turn of the century, water, sewer and park services in Boston were provided by separate regional commissions. That changed in 1919 with the formation of the Metropolitan District Commission (MDC), which took responsibility for the three services in the region. This move, nearly ninety years ago, was the first step in the creation of what was to become the Boston Harbor Islands National Park Area.

Rendering Plant and Garbage Dump

The islands were also put to new uses. The city of Boston purchased Apple's Island for use as a gravel pit. The island was renamed variously, Susana, Belle Isle and lastly, Breed's Island. (Apple Island was flattened out in 1946 to become part of Logan International Airport.) Moon Island, a forty-four acre island lying between Squantum section of the mainland and Long Island, was originally used for crops and livestock pasture. In 1878, the island was selected to become home to what was then considered the most modern sewage treatment and disposal system in the world. Here the city of Boston built a series of tunnels and massive granite settling tanks in the 1880s, which operated until the job was taken over by more advanced plants on Nut and Deer islands in the twentieth century.

Just before the Civil War, Nahum Ward paid fifteen thousand dollars for the failing hotel properties on Spectacle Island and then built a rendering plant on the island shortly after the war. The plant's purpose was to convert dead cattle and horses into usable products, such as hides, glues, horsehair and Neat's Foot Oil (a leather softener). The rendering plant served two purposes for the citizens of Boston—"preventative medicine" and "recycling." By removing the dead animal carcasses from the town, diseases were prevented from starting and becoming plagues. Through the manufacturing processes, animal parts were made into practical items for human use.

In 1888, Ward's plant was still operational with an entire community of families living on the island. According to the *King's Handbook*, there were thirty men employed and thirteen families living on the island. Vegetable gardens covered five acres and another thirty-seven acres were mowed. About seven thousand horses were received here yearly from points within ten miles to be made into hides, hair, oil, tallow and bone parts. A schoolhouse was constructed for children of the island families in 1882 and remained in operation until 1932.

In 1910, Nahum Ward's rendering plant closed because horse transportation was overtaken by the automobile and the market for products made from horses was diminishing. In 1912, a garbage-reclaiming dump was moved from Moon Island to Spectacle Island. The Boston Development and Sanitary Company ran the plant, whose purpose was to extract grease from garbage and sell it to soap manufacturers. The landfill from the garbage added five acres to the island and widened the sand bar connecting the two hills of Spectacle. In the 1930s, the market for reclaimed grease declined and the grease plant went out of business. Another company, Colman Disposal, continued to manage the garbage disposal operations there until 1955.

Until the island's extreme makeover in the late 1990s, the ruins of the grease extraction plant, particularly its dominant feature, a niney-foot draft chimney, could be seen well into the 1980s—hovering like a ghostly reminder of the island's earlier use.

Chapter 18

MARITIME TRADITION

Although the second half of the nineteenth century saw Boston transformed from a mercantile into a manufacturing city, it still looked seaward. Boston remained the nation's second most active port, second only to New York. And although Boston's wooden shipbuilding industry collapsed after the Civil War, the seaport retrenched and expanded. The Cunard Line and other packet lines began making regular sailings from Liverpool to Boston. As the downtown waterfront deteriorated, railroad companies moved in and built new port facilities in the rapidly expanding waterfront of South Bay and East Boston.

There they operated giant export grain and coal terminals backed by enormous railroad yards. On any given day, the harbor would be festooned with schooners, sloops, packets, brigantines and steamers carrying cargo from all over the world. A closer look at this beehive of activity would reveal among the tall ships smaller trawlers and dories of fishermen hauling their bounty from the sea. For many of the fishermen, especially many of Portuguese descent, Peddocks, Long, Calf, Great Brewster and Middle Brewster Islands were seasonal homes for their work.

Navigating Boston Harbor was and still is no mean feat. The harbor is comprised of some fifty square miles of unpredictable weather, of sudden squalls that turn calm waters into six-foot swells, of howling gales, northeasters and hurricanes that can pound ships against rocky ledges and capsize boats. It is a harbor where fogs sneak in, blanketing ships and shoals alike, leaving inexperienced navigators totally unaware of pending danger. It takes the most skilled skippers to navigate the Narrows, Black Rock Passage and Hypocrite Channel, their names as forbidding as the hidden underwater crags beneath these islands.

Indeed, Boston's maritime history reads like the obituary of the myriad ships that have met their watery fate off the islands of Boston Harbor. As early as the 1600s, shipwrecks have been recorded in Boston Harbor. There was the *Mary Rose*, a ten-gun, two-hundred-ton man-o'-war from Bristol, England, that was mysteriously "blown to pieces," killing all aboard, except one man, while anchored off Charlestown in 1640. In September 1697, the brig *Providence* struck Harding's Ledge and sunk while returning from Barbados, West Indies, with a cargo of rum. Down through the centuries, countless shipwrecks were recorded: the treasure-laden, French man-o'-war *Magnifique*, off Lovells Island; the *Lucretia*, off Deer Island; the *Midas*, off Georges Island; the list goes on and on.

Governor's Island and Fort Winthrop seen from Fort Independence ramparts, circa 1880. *Courtesy of the Metropolitan Commission District (MDC) archives.*

On the Middle Brewster. *Courtesy of* King's Handbook/*FBHI.*

The Graves. *Courtesy of Ron Goodman*.

In the second half of the nineteenth century, when many more ships made Boston their destination and better ship records were kept, fifty-eight shipwrecks were recorded. Two of the worst marine tragedies in Boston Harbor involved the *Maritana* and the *Portland*. In November of 1861, as the 990-ton, square-rigger *Maritana*, sailing from Liverpool approached Boston Harbor in a howling southeaster with blinding snow falling, the ship crashed into Shag Rocks, breaking the vessel in two. The captain and many of the crew and passengers died in the disaster. In a terrible storm in November, 1898—remembered as the "Portland Storm"—the steamship *Portland*, leaving the harbor crashed into Boston Light, leaving only a few survivors.

Among the more dramatic shipwreck rescues were the *Juliet* and the *Millie Trim*. When the granite-laden *Juliet* was wrecked in a storm off of Deer Island on January 9, 1886, inmates from the Deer Island prison rescued the crew and captain. On the same day and year, the *Millie Trim* plowed into Calf Island. According to one account, fishermen living on Calf Island saved the captain by rowing to his aid in a small dory, "a courageous act in turbulent surf."

With the growing congestion in the port of Boston (typically a hundred ships a day entered the harbor through Nantasket Roads, the main shipping channel), the increasing number of ship accidents and wrecks, and the perils of navigating the harbor came the growing need to construct navigational aids to guide ships through the often-treacherous waters. In addition to Boston Light on Little Brewster Island and Long Island Light on

Long Island, in the 1840s, a "telegraph" system utilizing signal flags was instituted in Boston to assist mariners and island residents in communicating with one another. From observatories located on Central Wharf and at the cupola of the Old State House, distress signals and calls for assistance could be seen.

In following years, Bug Light, standing at the entrance to the Narrows, was built in 1856 to warn mariners of the hidden sandbar, extending from Great Brewster under Black Rock Channel. The lighthouse was officially called the Narrows Lighthouse. (Locals called it Bug Light because the stilts supporting the lighthouse made it look like a giant bug with long legs.) In 1874, the federal government established the Lighthouse Buoy Station at Lovells Island where giant buoys were stored for instant service whenever the occasion demanded; and in 1890, Deer Island Light became operational. At the turn of the century, four range lights were built and activated on Spectacle Island to guide ships into Boston's inner harbor.

A few years later, Graves Light was built on a ledge of rocks at the entrance of the harbor to facilitate entering the newly opened Broad Sound Channel. The island is named for the seventeenth-century admiral Thomas Graves, but it is popularly associated with the "watery graves" surrounding it of numerous shipwrecks on and near its jagged rocks.

Chapter 19

URBAN NATURE

The rapid urbanization and industrialization of the United States in the second half of the nineteenth century brought a need for public spaces—the creation of urban parks, as park planners described it, "to satisfy physiological, social and psychological needs, giving relief from city air, noise and crowding…To provide a fresh-air setting for healthful exercise and a place for people to satisfy their human urge to mingle."

Frederick Law Olmsted, the famed landscape architect of Central Park in New York, was brought in to design an urban park system for Boston. In 1881, he designed what became known as the "Emerald Necklace," a winding corridor of pastoral parks connecting Boston's Back Bay Fens and running through the Fenway, Riverway and Jamaicaway along the Muddy River to a series of ponds and the Arnold Arboretum. Like Olmsted, Charles Eliot, who worked in Olmsted's landscape architectural firm, believed that particularly in crowded urban areas, people needed easy access to and contact with nature and open space in order to relax, unwind and escape the daily pressures of city life. To that end, Eliot developed a plan that would provide the growing city and its suburbs with scenery, parks and reservations to be held in perpetuity for the public's use and enjoyment.

By 1893, Eliot's design began to take shape as the state created the Metropolitan Parks Commission (MPC) and placed with it over nine thousand acres of reservation, thirteen miles of ocean frontage, fifty-six miles of riverbank and seven parkways. Collectively, however, the Boston Harbor Islands were not viewed as a recreational asset at that time. Diverse ownership, lack of easy access, and perhaps most importantly, the commercial importance of the waterfront directed pleasure-seeking crowds toward mainland resources. Nevertheless, Olmsted shared Eliot's vision of a system of green spaces where urban classes could mingle. He was intrigued with the recreational and aesthetic potential of the islands and the harbor, comparing Boston to Venice, Italy, in its appreciation for the waterfront.

Olmsted submitted a report proposing the reforestation of the Harbor Islands—not to create the picturesque landscape found in many parks and cemeteries at the time, but rather to restore the original forest cover of the islands. In environmental thinking decades ahead of his times, he suggested mixing fast-growing, reliable species, such as birch, with slower-growing native trees. The birch would mature faster and offer protection for developing species, allowing for a healthy forest canopy that would eventually replace the declining birch community.

The Boston Park Commission refused to appropriate funds for Olmsted's proposal for the Harbor Islands. Olmsted, nevertheless, kept pressing ahead on his plan to integrate the islands into an urban park. In the mid-1880s, municipal authorities requested that the federal government cede Castle Island back to Boston. Though the government initially refused, citing defense needs in the inner harbor, Boston acquired Castle Island, integrating the land surrounding Fort Independence into the nascent municipal park system in 1890. Olmsted's plan for the recreational use of Castle Island called for building a wooden pile bridge from South Boston to the island where "a continuous line of people, of many nationalities, mostly mothers and children, walking to and wandering the island, enjoying the cool, invigorating seas breezes" would be welcomed. The transformation of Castle Island into a recreational area complemented Eliot's idea to set aside beachfront along the bay and land along the Charles, Mystic and Neponset Rivers, turning these properties into regional parks.

Despite the lack of early municipal management, the Harbor Islands remained a popular recreational destination. One of the favorite recreational uses of the islands was to enjoy them from the deck of a sightseeing steamboat. "Numerous steamboats ply between the city and places of resort in the harbor and just outside of it," observed one contemporary writer. "For reasonable fees one may steam in and out between the several islands, and enjoy, on the most sultry of days, a cool and refreshing breeze, together with the most delightful and ever-changing scenery."

According to the Cultural Landscape Report for the Boston Harbor Islands, prepared by the Olmsted Center for Preservation for the National Park Service, Boston, December 2001:

> Swimming, yachting and motor-boating were popular along the harbor coast of the industrial city. Boston Yacht Club, the first regular local club, was organized in 1865. The South Boston and Lynn clubs followed three years later. During the next fifteen years, clubs were established at Quincy, Dorchester, Charlestown, Chelsea, East Boston, and Winthrop. Hull Yacht Club, founded in 1882, was the second largest club in the country, nearly 500 members by the end of the century. At the turn of the century Massachusetts Bay was probably the greatest yachting center in the country, and many avid boaters planned day-excursions to the islands in Boston Harbor."

Island Residences

In 1855, Boston businessman John Brewer purchased ten acres on Cushing's Neck in Hingham for a summer residence. By 1882, Brewer's holdings included World's End, Planter's Hill and Cushing's Neck—all told, a 248-acre peninsula of rolling fields and five miles of rugged shoreline jutting out into Hingham Bay. On the land was Brewer's huge wood-shingled mansion and sprawling farm that included stables, barns, blacksmith shop, greenhouse, poultry house, workers' quarters and windmills. Prize Jersey cattle grazed on the rolling pastureland. On the hillside grew fields of hay, corn, oats, sugar beets, alfalfa and vegetables. During this time, Brewer also acquired Sarah and Langlee Islands in Hingham Harbor.

Above: View of Castle Island from South Boston. *Courtesy of Massachusetts Bicentennial Commission.*

Right: Boston Yacht Club, City Point. *Courtesy of* King's Handbook/*FBHI.*

Nut Island, Boston Harbor Islands National Park Area   Managed by the Massachusetts Water Resources Authority

When Houghs Neck was a popular summer resort in the late 1800s and early 1900s, holidaymakers picnicked on Nut Island and swam here in Hingham Bay. Many summer residents built cottages nearby using windows, doors, and hardware salvaged from ships that were dismantled here. A harbor within a harbor, Hingham Bay is once again a recreational treasure on the edge of the city and the ocean.

Hingham Bay

Postcards from the early 1900s show (clockwise from top left) the Pandora Hotel, the Old Nut Island pumping station, Houghs Neck shoreline and yacht club. *Courtesy of MWRA.*

In 1886, Brewer hired Olmsted to draw up a park plan for his estate. The plan included subdividing Planter's Hill and World's End, probably intending a suburban development, rather than a summer community, in case it became financially necessary to sell part of his land. Gravel paths—lined with oak, hickory and red cedar trees, and following the contour of the land—were constructed, transforming World's End (the name now given for the entire area) into a New England version of the Elysian Fields. Committed to the reforestation of the Boston Harbor Islands, Olmsted also called for the tree-planting program to be extended to Sarah and Langlee Islands.

The Brewer family line died out in 1936. Eventually the cows were sold and the buildings were torn down. But trustees of the estate managed to protect the land against urban encroachment and the construction of a nuclear power plant until 1967. At that time, with the threat of development growing, the present owners, the Trustees of Reservations, a private Massachusetts conservation organization, stepped in to purchase the land to protect and preserve it for public enjoyment.

Augustus Russ was another wealthy resident of the Harbor Islands. In the mid-1870s, Russ, the founder of the Boston Yacht Club, purchased Middle Brewster Island, a high, twelve-acre outcrop, from resident fishermen and built a tall white summer villa perched on the southwestern cliff of the island. Many wealthy Bostonians were known to enjoy a day of yachting and a night of entertainment at Russ's villa. "Here the patrician yachtsman and other guests enjoy ease with dignity during the dog-days, and are entertained with free hospitality at the Russ villa," noted a contemporary observer.

The most opulent residence was on Calf Island, a flat seventeen-acre rock mass island situated north of Great Brewster Island. Benjamin P. Cheney, a noted yachtsman and railroad financier, and his wife, actress Julia Arthur, had spent several summers in a little house on Middle Brewster. When Cheney wanted to build an icehouse, Russ refused his request to put up an additional building on his property. Rather than become embroiled in a property-rights dispute, Cheney decided to buy his own island. So he bought Calf Island and in 1902, he built a large estate on the southeastern cliffs and planned both a swimming pool and golf links on the grounds. "A little village in itself," the estate, known as "The Moorings" included a two-story colonial-style villa, a large boathouse and servants' quarters. Stone stairs led from the boat landing to a belvedere with views toward Boston and up to the estate.

Julia Arthur was at that time one of the most distinguished American actresses in this country and abroad. She scored her greatest successes in contemporary drama in her portrayal of famed Shakespearean women. Particularly known for her highly-geared temperament, she once said in an interview: "Emotional roles are the ones I succeed best with; those that require pathos, yes, and tears, for I believe, all that is said to the contrary notwithstanding, that people like to have their sympathies touched; women especially like to go to the theatre to see plays that make them cry." Arthur played the leading feminine roles in about two hundred plays, including "The Lady of Lyons," "East Lynne," "Don Caesar de Bazan," "The Corsican Brothers," "The Galley Slave," "Women Against Women," "Lady Windemere's Fan" and "More Than Queen."

In her autobiography *My Career*, Arthur reminisced about her days on Calf Island. Overworked and exhausted, Arthur had fainted on stage during a performance in New York City. Her cure was to rest and to enjoy complete freedom from anxiety and the tranquility of a home atmosphere.

> *At first we lived quietly in the Cheney cottage at Middle Brewster, Massachusetts, and before the novelty of that environment could wear off, Mr. Cheney launched me into the delights of building a home of our own. For this we chose an ideal setting—Calf Island, in Boston Harbor, where we could live a life of splendid isolation if we chose, or leave it abruptly and within an hour be again in the heart of the city.*
>
> *To insure our isolation we bought the island, and to provide the needed excitement of existence we set up a small fleet of boats, of which the most ambitious is the* Jule. *Incidentally, in building the house we had all the thrills that usually attend this experiment, as well as a few unusual ones we threw in for good measure. Several times we were marooned on the island by sudden storms. Occasionally we had mishaps in our boats.*
>
> *Life was not monotonous. Part of our boathouse, by the way, was the deck of a ship that was washed ashore more than fifty years ago; and we were careful to make the house and grounds fit their splendid setting of sea and sky. We called the place "the Moorings," and after a very little time there my old life on the stage began to seem vague and dreamlike—almost as if I had lived it on some other wandering planet.*

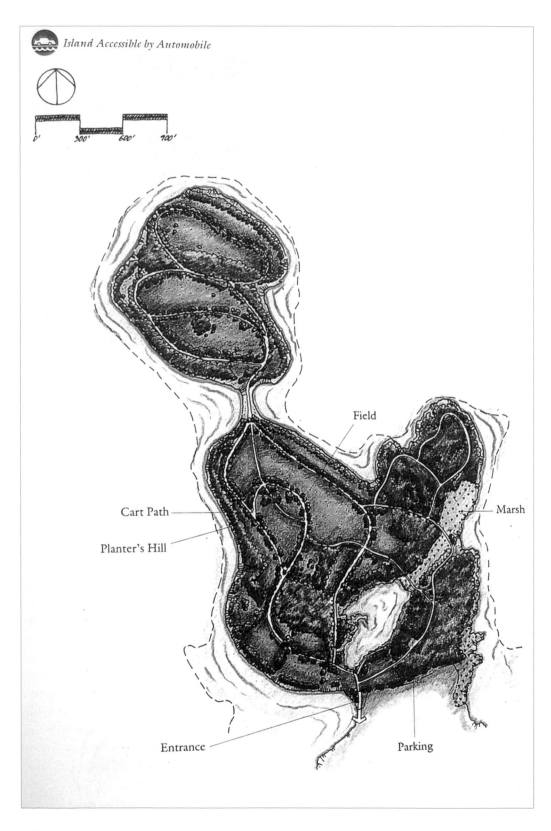

Island Accessible by Automobile

0' 300' 600' 900'

Field

Cart Path

Planter's Hill

Marsh

Entrance

Parking

Right: Villa of Augustine Russ on Middle Brewster. *Courtesy of* King's Handbook */FBHI.*

Opposite: World's End. *Courtesy of NPS.*

'The Moorings' required a lot of work, and the best way to get that work out of other persons, I soon found, was to understand it myself. We had a big place. There was no telephone communication with the mainland, so our marketing had to be done by boat. We were nine miles from a lemon and from every other household necessity. We spent our summers at 'The Moorings' for twelve years—going there in June, leaving the last of September, and filling it during the interval with our families and closest friends.

Julia Arthur died on March 30, 1950. She asked that her ashes be committed to Boston Harbor.

The United States government acquired rights to the island during the First World War and the estate was abandoned. Cheney's imposing estate was destroyed by fire, set probably by vandals, after World War II. All that remains today is the ruins of a chimney that stands like a ghost over the foundation of the once-great estate.

Chinese Picnics

While the popularity of recreating on the Boston Harbor Islands continued to grow in the second half of the nineteenth century, it was increasingly of a different nature. Wealthy Bostonians were now searching out more distant and exotic destinations, abandoning the islands to illicit pleasure-seekers who took advantage of the islands' seclusion and its proximity to Boston to watch unsanctioned boxing matches and baseball games, gamble, take drugs and have sex, as prostitution rings were set up on the islands.

" *My Career* "
by
Julia Arthur

Courtesy of Hull Lifesaving Museum.

Fishing parties were replaced by "Chinese picnics"—the euphemistic name for opium parties. Long Island was said to have attracted "adventurous young men" and "a large assemblage of bruisers and plug-uglies" to illegal events. Eventually the law intruded into the illegal activities that took place on Long Island. On June 29, 1873, the police launched a raid to stop an illegal prizefight on the island. It was the beginning of police crackdowns there.

Spectacle Island met a similar fate. Although the two hotels built there in 1847 flourished as respectable resorts in their early years, they soon slipped into such illegal activities as gambling and prostitution. A police raid in 1858 to close the premises led to their bankruptcy shortly after.

From the late nineteenth century through the early twentieth century, there were two inns on Peddocks Island: The Island Inn, owned by John Irwin; and the Y.O. West End House, owned by W.L. Drake. Although Bostonians may have patronized the inns for their deviled lobsters for seventy-five cents, clam chowder for twenty cents, French fried potatoes for fifteen cents and a bottle of Guinness for thirty cents, they would have more likely made the trip to Peddocks to partake in a Chinese picnic or watch an illegal boxing match or baseball game.

The Boston Braves National League team was prohibited to play baseball in its stadium on Sunday because of Boston's Blue Laws. John Irwin, the proprietor of the Island Inn and a former professional baseball player, managed to circumvent the law by getting the Braves to play their Sunday games on Peddocks. Boats would typically bring over five thousand spectators to these Sunday ballgames. A Chinese picnic on July 29, 1909, did not have a pleasant ending. According to the *Boston Herald*, the chief of police of Hull arrested Irwin in an attempt to bring a stop to the illegal recreational activities on Peddocks. Irwin was taken to Hull, where bail was placed at two hundred dollars. A bondsman put up the bail and Irwin was freed. Little is known as to what happened to Irwin afterwards. A few years later, though, the two inns on Peddocks shut down.

As the nineteenth century came to a close, the city saw the need to step in and "clean up" the islands. Police raids became more frequent and the popularity of a summer day excursion to the islands declined. But it was the Spanish-American War in 1898 and subsequently, World Wars I and II, when the islands were once again used for defense, that effectively ended most recreational activity—both legal and illegal—on the islands for the greater part of the twentieth century.

Bird's-eye view of Boston Harbor, circa 1920s. *Courtesy of BPL.*

Chapter 20

THE TWENTIETH CENTURY

After the Civil War, the advances in weapons technology and the experience gained from naval attacks against land fortifications ended the time-honored axiom that ships could not successfully attack a properly located and manned land fort. Accelerating progress in metallurgy, explosives, ballistics and communications created steam-powered steel warships, more maneuverable and mounted with guns equal to the firepower of a fort. The brick and granite walls of the forts would crumble under the pounding of the shells from the ships' improved guns. Defensively, the modern ships' iron- and steel-clad hulls were protected from the round shot of the smoothbore Rodman cannons that were used in the Civil War and are now obsolete.

Recognizing the need to upgrade the nation's coastal defenses, the Endicott Board was established in 1888. Chaired by Secretary of War William Endicott, who was from Salem, Massachusetts, the Endicott Board set forth policies and plans for the defense of the Atlantic seaboard. The Board recommended that Boston Harbor be defended by 175 modern guns and mortars. Fort Warren on Georges Island was selected for the role of central fire control for all the harbor fortifications. The first step in the plan called for submarine mines to be placed in the channels where they could be detonated by electrical cables connected to controls in a small bombproof casement at Fort Warren.

Following the guidelines of the Endicott Board, the War Department took over Long Island Head on Long Island and an area in Winthrop, which it designated Fort Banks, thus bracketing the harbor with fortifications. Construction began on seven other forts in Boston Harbor: Fort Heath (along with Fort Banks) on Winthrop Heights; Fort Revere, Nantasket Head; Fort Strong, Long Island; Fort Standish, Lovells Island; Fort Warren, Georges Island; and Fort Andrews, Peddocks Island. Fort Winthrop on Governor's Island and Fort Independence on Castle Island were relegated to secondary status. Fort Independence was used as depot for submarine mines.

The forts were constructed of a new material—reinforced concrete, replacing the old brick and granite walls of earlier fortifications. The guns were emplaced in subterranean bunkers or pits, with walls of concrete fifteen to twenty feet thick that were covered by earth to give an added protective thickness. Batteries of two to four guns, ranging in size from three- and five-inch to ten-, twelve-, and thirteen-inch guns were constructed around the fort. Many of the batteries consisted of state-of-the-art "disappearing guns."

(They were called "disappearing guns" because the guns were visible over the parapet when firing, with the recoil causing it to disappear into a recessed area behind.)

The seven forts in Boston Harbor were still under construction when on February 15, 1898, the battleship *Maine* mysteriously exploded in Havana Harbor, igniting the spark that set off the Spanish-American War. "Remember the Maine!" became the rallying cry for the country that was for war against Spain—a war stoked largely by newspaper stories of Spain's brutal suppression of a colonial rebellion in Cuba.

In their battle for market share, American newspapers, particularly William Randolph Hearst's *New York Journal*, resorted to "yellow journalism," featuring startling headlines, lurid stories and abuse of the facts to attract readers. A classic example of yellow journalism was the exchange between Hearst and the artist Frederick Remington, who had been sent by the *Journal* to sketch some pictures of Spanish atrocities. When Remington cabled his publisher that all was quiet in Cuba and asked if he could come home, Hearst replied: "Please remain...You furnish the pictures and I'll furnish the war."

With the country now fired up and clamoring for war, President McKinley sent a message to Congress asking it to support "forcible intervention" to establish peace in Cuba. Spain interpreted this as a declaration of war. It was. On April 24, 1898, the United States declared war on Spain. Less than twenty-four hours later, Boston was bolstering its harbor defenses. With fewer than 250 officers and men stationed at Boston Harbor Island batteries, the First Regiment of Massachusetts Artillery was marching down to Rowe's Wharf where the men embarked on the *General Lincoln* to Fort Warren. Soon, other units were moving out to island forts.

Immediately upon declarations of war, Boston became concerned that it would be attacked by the Spanish. Newspapers headlined stories convincing the public that Spanish Admiral Cervera and his "spook-fleets" were lurking offshore. Rumors spread that the Spanish flotilla had left the Cape Verde Islands on April 29 for an unknown destination—was it Boston? It was said that there was a public banquet in Havana to celebrate the bombardment of Boston.

Reports out of the harbor seemed to support the rumors. Fort sentinels often mistook the masts of friendly fishing crafts and coastal schooners for the dreaded Spanish fleet. On one occasion, a sentinel at Fort Warren saw four ships in single file approaching the fort at night. The sentinel thought that the Spanish fleet was approaching, because he saw lights blinking like signals between enemy ships. It turned out to be a tug towing barges. On another occasion, an engineer boat arrived, whistle shrieking, at the Fort Warren pier, with intelligence from the Boston Navy Yard that the Spanish fleet would attack Boston the next day. Fort Warren went on full alert; but the Spanish never came. Admiral Cervera's fleet was destroyed outside Santiago Harbor, Cuba, on July 3, 1898. On the same day, Teddy Roosevelt led a charge up San Juan Hill that scattered Spanish defenders.

Hostilities were suspended and a peace protocol was signed on August 13. Through victory in this "Splendid Little War," almost overnight, America had become a colonial power with the annexation of the Philippines, Puerto Rico and several Pacific islands.

1880s garrison inspection at Fort Independence, unchanged since the Civil War. *Courtesy of United States Army Military History Institute/Gerald Butler.*

Gun drill, 10-inch disappearing rifle, Battery Hitcock–Ward, Fort Strong, Long Island, circa 1917. *Courtesy of MDC archives.*

In the spring of 1899, Castle Island, which was restricted when war broke out, was once again opened as a public park. Fort Independence was stripped of most of its guns, and by 1900, relegated to caretaker status. Because the war was so brief, construction of many of the harbor fortifications was unfinished before war's end. A military reservation was designated for Lovells Island; but it wasn't until 1900 that installation of the island's seven gun batteries was completed and the reservation officially designated Fort Standish, in honor of Miles Standish, the first military commander of the Plymouth Colony. On the eve of World War I, the defense plan envisioned by the Endicott Board for the islands of Boston Harbor was completed. The harbor's defenses were ready for war once again.

THE FIRST WORLD WAR

Unlike its harbor defenses before the Spanish-American War, Boston's island fortifications were ready for action with the advent of World War I. According to Gerald Butler, who chronicles the history of Boston's fortifications in *The Guns of Boston Harbor*, immediately following President Wilson's declaration of war in April, 1917, "sentinels were posted at the wooden bridge to Castle Island, along the seawall, and in Fort Independence...A small wooden observation post from which the whole harbor could be scrutinized was built atop Bastion B. Circular concrete pads for anti-aircraft guns were constructed on Bastions D and E." The fort was primarily used to store small arms ammunition, which were transshipped to Europe.

On Deer Island, personnel from coast artillery units and regular army staff were moved to the island to man an observation station and conduct foot patrols, watching for any approaching danger. From a hill, two sixty-inch searchlights swept the main channel looking for possible enemy submarines entering the port. Troop strength at Fort Standish on Lovells Island, which consisted of a small militia encampment before the war, was bolstered by elements of the First Coast Command and regular army personnel arriving on the island shortly after war was declared.

Fort Warren on Georges Island was the headquarters for the coast defense of Boston. Troops began arriving on the island shortly after war was declared, and by December of 1917, 1,600,000 men were quartered at the fort and scattered in tents set up throughout the island. Most of the soldiers were from the Fifty-fifth Coast Artillery, which was made up of eight companies from Boston and vicinity. One of the first tasks of the troops was to lay minefields and submarine nets across Nantasket Roads channel and the Narrows, between Georges and Lovells Islands. Unfortunately, the mines and nets were carried away by severe storms that began in December of 1917, rendering the system ineffectual until it could be repaired the following spring.

Conditions inside Fort Warren were grueling. "Ice prevented food deliveries, the granite chambers overflowed with personnel, and cases of mild hypothermia and frostbite kept the medical staff busy," wrote Butler. On March 8, 1918, a notification announced that Boston Harbor was placed "under quarantine on account of the prevalence of scarlet fever; and no one was allowed, not even the officers, to go on pass." The notification was a ruse, planted by military intelligence to mislead German spies to thinking the troops were to be really quarantined in Boston Harbor. Instead, on March 18, the Fifty-fifth Coast Artillery were transported from Georges Island to Commonwealth Pier in Boston, where they boarded troop trains bound to New York. From New York, the Fifty-fifth sailed to France, serving in the American First Army.

Troop strength was also increased at Fort Strong on Long Island. Coastal artillery units were added to regular army personnel and state militia units that preceded them shortly after war was declared. Temporary barracks were quickly built to house the growing number of troops assigned to the overcrowded fort. The rapid troop expansion caused a shortage of food and provisions, which had to be rationed in what troops referred to as the "ice blockade" when the harbor froze over, crippling deliveries. Butler said that firewood scavengers would comb the shore for driftwood until ice prevented flotsam. Then they started cutting down trees and thick brush on the island until the commanding officer ordered the scavengers to stop or "by the end of winter the island would be bare of growth."

Fort Andrews on Peddocks Island housed one of the largest harbor garrisons. Massive brick barracks lining the main thoroughfare from the pier to the mortar batteries housed the nearly two thousand troops stationed on the island. Fort Andrews suffered the same shortages of food and fuel to the ice blockade as the other harbor island forts. At one point, Butler said "all supplies were rationed and Navy destroyers had to break a path through the harbor ice to supply Fort Andrews in that frigid winter of 1917–1918." In March, 1918, units of the Fifty-fifth Coast Artillery departed Peddocks Island for the campaigns of Aisne-Marne, Champagne, Oise-Aisne and Meuse-Argonne, "earning commendations on the accuracy of their shooting, including one incident in which they destroyed a bridge five miles behind the German lines with only three 155-mm shells."

There were other wartime uses of the Harbor Islands, as well. Bumpkin Island, which had been used as a children's hospital prior to the war, was purchased by the navy for training and a naval hospital. At its peak during 1918, over 1,300 sailors were stationed on the island, quartered in fifty-eight buildings. On Gallops Island, German sailors, who were interned on ships in Boston Harbor, were transferred to the island as POWs.

After the Armistice was signed on November 11, 1918, the forts on the Boston Harbor Islands were downsized the following year to their pre-war status. Fort Strong reverted to maintenance status. Fort Warren also reverted to maintenance status and headquarters of the Coast Defenses of Boston was transferred to Fort Banks on Governor's Island. The garrison at Fort Andrews was reduced and then removed. The guns and carriages of batteries at Fort Standish were dismounted. Castle Island reverted to a city park with Fort Independence reduced to caretaker status.

Before the war ended, though, another scourge swept through Boston Harbor that would take a toll in human lives far greater than the Great War itself.

The Influenza Pandemic of 1918

In the summer of 1918, Boston was a busy port. Troops and shipments of machinery and supplies were arriving and leaving the port, their final destination—the Western Front. On August 28, eight sailors, who were on a ship docked at Commonwealth Pier

Fort Andrews, Peddocks Island, 1917. *Courtesy of U.S. Army Military History Institute/Gerald Butler.*

on the Boston waterfront, came down with the flu. The next day, fifty-eight were sick and the toll kept rising. In a week, 119 were sick. Deaths soon followed. On September 8, three people died from the flu in Boston. On that same day, the flu appeared at Fort Devens, an army base thirty miles west of Boston. Within twenty-four hours after its first appearance, sixty-three soldiers were dead. Almost overnight, the flu went on a rampage, spreading through the base built to house thirty-five thousand, but overcrowded with fifty thousand military personnel. The hospital, built to hold two thousand sick, was overflowing with eight thousand patients. A government medical officer described coming into the hospital's wards and seeing soldiers placed on cots, "their faces wear a blush cast; a distressing cough brings up the blood-stained sputum. In the morning, the dead bodies are stacked about the morgue like cordwood."

By September 1918, as many as 50,000 people in Massachusetts had the flu; more than 120 Bostonians had died of it; with 33 more succumbing to pneumonia-related contagion. Things got so bad that Massachusetts officials asked state Governor Calvin Coolidge to go to President Wilson, pleading for more doctors and nurses to help battle the flu. But no more help could be diverted to Massachusetts. The flu had spread throughout military bases and towns and cities throughout the nation—twelve thousand people across the country had already died of influenza.

It was called the Boston Experiment. In the search to find a way to combat the deadly flu, a group of navy doctors came up with a plan. Sixty-two sailors from the U.S. Navy Training Station on Deer Island were in trouble. Each had been convicted and imprisoned for crimes committed while in the service. In November 1918, the Navy made these prisoners an offer they couldn't refuse. If they agreed to be subjects in a medical study that might help scientists understand how the flu was spread and if they agreed to allow doctors to give them the potentially deadly disease, in return, they would be pardoned for their crimes.

The sailors, none of whom had the flu, were transferred to the quarantine station on Gallops Island. There, navy doctors did their best to give the men the flu. Mucus was collected from men sick with the flu and sprayed into the noses and throats of the prisoners. The thinking was that the influenza was a respiratory disease, spread from person to person. Presumably, it was carried on droplets of mucus sprayed in the air when sick people coughed or sneezed; or carried on their hands and spread when the sick touched the healthy. Not a single sailor in the experiment contracted the flu, however. The sailors got their pardons; but the Boston Experiment failed to discover any solution to the devastating disease.

Known as the "Spanish Flu," the influenza of 1918 was a global disaster, cited as the most devastating epidemic in world history. It is estimated that between 20 and 40 million people died from the influenza. (Some estimate that the total of all those killed worldwide as high as 100 million.) Before it vanished in eighteen months, the Spanish Flu claimed more lives than the Black Death Bubonic Plague from 1347 to 1351. (AIDs killed 25 million in its first twenty-five years; the Spanish Flu killed as many in only twenty-five weeks beginning in September, 1918.) In two years, this scourge ravaged the earth; a fifth of the world's population was infected.

It infected 28 percent of all Americans, mysteriously hitting many more people between the ages of twenty to forty than the elderly or young. An estimated 675,000 Americans died of influenza during the pandemic, ten times as many as in the World War. Of the U.S. soldiers who died in Europe, half of them fell to the influenza virus and not to the enemy. An estimated forty-three thousand servicemen mobilized for World War I died of influenza.

Death by the virus was rapid and frequently hideous. People without symptoms could be struck suddenly and be rendered too feeble to walk within hours; many would die the next day. Symptoms included a blue tint to the face and coughing up blood caused by severe obstruction of the lungs. In further stages, the virus caused an "uncontrollable hemorrhaging that filled the lungs and patients would drown in their own bodily fluids, struggling to clear the airways of a blood-tinged froth that gushed from their nose and mouth" as one physician described the death throes.

The influenza pandemic circled the globe. It spread following the path of its human carriers, along trade routes and shipping lines. Outbreaks swept through North America, Europe, Asia, Africa, Brazil and the South Pacific. In India, the mortality rate was extremely high, at around fifty deaths from influenza per thousand people. The Great War, with its mass movements of men in America and aboard ships, probably aided in its rapid diffusion and attack.

The origins of the deadly flu disease were unknown but widely speculated upon. Some of the allies thought of the epidemic as a biological warfare tool of the Germans. Many thought it was a result of the trench warfare, the use of mustard gases and the generated "smoke and fumes" of the war. A national campaign began using the ready rhetoric of war to fight "the new enemy of microscopic proportions." As the *Journal of the American Medical Association* noted in its final edition of 1918:

> *1918 has gone: A year momentous as the termination of the most cruel war in the annals of the human race; a year which marked, the end at least for a time, of man's destruction of man; unfortunately a year in which developed a most infectious disease causing the death of hundreds of thousands of human beings. Medical science for four and one-half years devoted itself to putting men on the firing line and keeping them there. Now it must turn with its whole might to combating the greatest enemy of all—infectious disease.*

Where the Spanish Flu originated is not precisely known—maybe it was China. The name, Spanish Flu, came from the early affliction and large number of mortalities in Spain, where it allegedly killed 8 million in May of 1918. However, a first wave of influenza appeared earlier in the spring at Fort Riley, Kansas, and in other military camps throughout the United States. Few noticed the epidemic in the midst of the war. There was virtually no response or acknowledgement to the epidemic in March and April in the military camps. But in hindsight, these first incidents of the epidemic at training camps were a sign of what was coming in greater magnitude in the fall and winter of 1918 to the entire world.

Troops returning from Europe brought the virus back into the United States for the second wave. The port of entry for the deadly disease was Boston, August 1918.

Chapter 21

BETWEEN THE WORLD WARS

The Great War sharply stimulated American patriotism and caused a xenophobia of Germans. After the war, the wartime fear of Germans transmuted into a fear and suspicion of all foreigners. The country was on edge. Labor violence and strikes were spreading among the workers of America. The 1917 Russian Revolution reinforced a growing suspicion toward foreigners as the Bolsheviks took power in what was called a proletarian revolution, striking fear in the hearts of capitalists everywhere that their own workers might follow the Russian example.

As Bolshevism in Russia hardened into tyranny, American newspapers and magazines trumpeted over and over again the terrifying theme of "It must not happen here." Employers who once had welcomed the influx of cheap and docile foreign workers now became frightened by local labor unrest and by what appeared to be the spreading threat of a new and dangerously radical spirit in Europe.

In September 1919, the violence and labor unrest struck Boston. The Boston police went on strike igniting two days of violence and looting before some five thousand National Guardsmen restored order. Massachusetts governor Calvin Coolidge, who had done little to prevent the police strike, then sent a telegram to the American Federation of Labor's (AFL) Samuel Gompers stating "There is no right to strike against public safety of anybody, anywhere and anytime." Coolidge's hard-line position resounded throughout the country as it brought him national recognition and later catapulted him to the presidency.

Later in the month, federal troops were sent to quiet the nation's steel towns, and in November, when 394,000 coal miners left the pits, the public feared this was the beginning of a nationwide general strike, or worse. The close alliance of anti-foreign sentiment with the fear of radical labor activity swelled to a national hysteria known as "The Red Scare."

Riding the tide of the Red Scare and having his own political ambitions, A. Mitchell Palmer, President Wilson's attorney general, first in November, 1919, then again in January, 1920, launched a series of lightning-like raids on private houses and public buildings across the United States. To become known as the Palmer Raids, federal agents of the Department of Justice, with the help of local police forces, carried out these raids

Shirley Gut, which once separated Winthrop from Deer Island. Deer Island prison is in the background (to the left). *Courtesy of MWRA.*

against all radical groups, or who were perceived as radicals—communists, anarchists, Industrial Workers of the World (IWW)—"with great brutality and violence."

Union headquarters were raided, equipment smashed, literature seized and people, especially foreigners, beaten up and arrested. The thousands arrested, many of whom were American citizens with no connections with communism, were held unjustifiably in jail or deported in an anti-Red campaign that proved to be the most serious infringement of civil liberties since the nation's early years. The raids were particularly intense and violent in the industrial towns around Boston and culminated, according to one newspaper account, in "captives being driven through the streets of Boston chained together in fours."

After being beaten and put through the third degree, the prisoners were sent to Deer Island in Boston Harbor—the same island where over 240 years before, Native Americans captured in King Philip's War were imprisoned. More than four hundred were rounded up from New England and jammed into the underheated and overcrowded Deer Island prison. There in the next few weeks one of them went insane, another jumped to his death from the fifth floor of the main block and several others attempted suicide. When they were finally released, as most of them were, many were ill and showed signs of beating. A federal judge later ironically praised the "experimental prison self-government" of the many foreign-born workers imprisoned there as the "Soviet Republic of Deer Island."

By February 1919, lawyers across the country were speaking out on Palmer's misuse of federal power and his raiders' violation of Constitutional rights. By the spring of 1920, Palmer's anti-Red Scare campaign had subsided. Palmer had predicted that 2,720 aliens from the raids would be deported; in the end only 556 were. In all, more than four thousand suspects were released. The Red Scare was over. The country returned to normalcy.

The decades between the two World Wars saw the islands of Boston Harbor return to many of their pre-war uses. Castle Island reverted to its use as a city park; but it became an island in name only. Over the years, the area between the island and the mainland had been filled in by hydraulic dredging, and by the mid-1920s, the land had settled sufficiently to allow construction of a rough dirt road and concrete walk to replace a wooden bridge. In 1932, a new roadway, now called the William J. Day Boulevard, was opened with a large rotary in sight of Fort Independence.

On Long Island, during the 1920s and 1930s, new buildings, roadways and wharves were added to the chronic disease hospital, which was built at the turn of the century. At its height, the hospital complex housed more than 1,225 almshouse inmates and 450 patients. During the Great Depression, a farm, cattle pasture and piggery operated on the island. (During the 1930s, Olmsted's vision for the islands of Boston Harbor was partially and temporarily realized. The Civilian Conservation Corps (CCC) planted about a hundred thousand pine trees on the Harbor Islands in 1934. Unfortunately, many of these seedlings were removed with the reactivation of the islands' military installations during World War II.)

In 1900, the Boston Asylum and Farm School on Thompson Island was renamed the Boston Farm and Trade School. In the 1920s, new buildings were added and a new curriculum was introduced, offering boys academic courses and making it possible to enter the second or third year of high school. At the same time, farm work and agricultural training became less of a focus. James Longley, a wealthy financier and Boston philanthropist, was a major impetus behind the change. Longley had a special attraction to the Boston Farm and Trade School. When he died in 1917, Longley bequeathed $150,000 to the school that enabled it to adapt to the educational needs of the twentieth century. By 1941, the school had become a six-year secondary school (officially renamed Thompson Academy in 1956, it is now closed). The farm program was eliminated and students began wearing coats and ties.

Many of the islands had summer residences throughout the 1920s and 1930s. From 1900 until 1941, fifteen families leased summer cottages on Great Brewster Island from the federal government. Among the summer cottagers were colorful characters, such as Frank McKinley, "Shanghai Harry" Long, Ray Thomas, and "Joe Peg-Leg" Neskey. On Peddocks Island, Portuguese fishermen occupied cottages forming a summer community on the island's East Head. Additional cottages were constructed on Middle Head during these years. A number of these cottages continue to be seasonally occupied to this day.

Several other islands had recreational uses during these years. Sheep Island harbored a private residence and hunting lodge until the mid-1900s. On Raccoon Island, a three-acre bedrock outcropping just off Hough's Neck in Quincy, the Stigmatine Religious

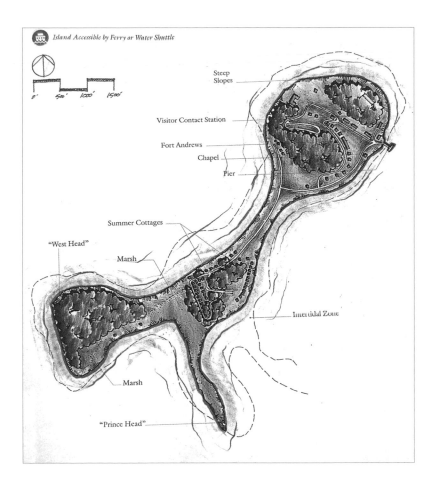

Peddocks Island.
Courtesy of NPS.

Order operated a summer camp for boys in the 1930s. And fishermen, like the Native Americans of long ago, were known to have summered on Green Island until the last house on the island burned down in 1932.

RUMRUNNING, BOOTLEGGING AND PROHIBITION

The Roaring Twenties was a flamboyant decade—an age of unabashed materialism, revolution in morals, and Prohibition (1920–1933). The hip flask, filled with illicit, or "bootleg" whiskey, was the symbol of the era. Every community of any size had its "speakeasies," where homemade and imported alcoholic beverages could be bought. Keeping the speakeasies supplied was an occupation for many thousands of bootleggers, beer barons and rumrunners who worked beyond the law.

Often their rivalries and differences of opinions resulted in open warfare and gangland slayings. Rumrunning originated at the start of Prohibition when ships from the nearby island of Bimini transported cheap Caribbean rum to Florida speakeasies. But rum's cheapness made it low-profit for the rumrunners, and they soon moved to smuggling Canadian whisky, French champagne and English gin to major cities like New York and Boston, where prices ran high. It was said that some ships carried two hundred thousand dollars in contraband in a single run—at a time when fifty dollars a week was considered a good wage for an honest worker.

As the profits from rumrunning grew, it attracted many legitimate businessmen, including Joseph P. Kennedy Sr., father of the future president, who purportedly financed rum-running operations from Canada and represented several British alcohol distillers. Large profits also attracted businessmen who were less legitimate, and it was not long before the mob got involved. Organized crime had no experienced seamen, however, so their involvement was largely in transporting the produce from the dock to the speakeasies and running the clubs.

The mob was also handy in bribery and blackmail. Many a police officer or watchman was "convinced" to be absent when a certain boat docked and was unloaded. Policemen in the 1920s made between twenty and forty dollars a week, and an envelope with a few twenties, or a portion of the cargo, went a long way. In Boston, the mafia was a small, insignificant organization run by Gaspare Messina from 1916 to1924. The real criminal power in the city was a South Boston Irishman named Frankie Wallace, leader of the Gustin Gang, until the Italians assassinated him in the North End in 1931. After that day, there was finally enough room for the Italian Mafia, confined to the North End, to expand and prosper.

Following the Gustin Gang's demise, Boston organized crime was a loose confederation of ethnic racketeers and bootleggers. One of the earliest figures in New England's criminal history was Charles "King" Solomon. Reigning over Jewish criminal operations, Solomon controlled the majority of illegal gambling before expanding into bootlegging during Prohibition. Attending the Atlantic City Conference in 1927, Solomon was one of several leaders who helped negotiate territorial disputes and establish policies that would influence the later National Crime Syndicate in 1932.

King Solomon continued to control illegal gambling in New England until his reign was over in January, 1933, when he was gunned down in front of Boston's Cotton Club by Irish gangsters. From that moment, Boston's criminal landscape was dramatically altered. A former Sicilian fight promoter named Fillippo "Phil" Buccula ultimately gained the upper hand in the Boston Mafia over Joseph Lombardo, taking over bootlegging operations in the area, and ruling a small but lean family until 1954.

Bootlegging was not only big business in Boston Harbor, but small business on the Harbor Islands as well. Old timers from South Boston recount stories of people boating out to Rainsford Island, "where currents washed up bootlegged cargoes dumped overboard as the Coast Guard ships approached." Another South Boston native told about his father's cellar still. Matilda Silvia, a long time resident of Peddocks Island until her death in 2003, wrote in her memoirs *Once Upon An Island* that she could see the rum-running boats docked at the army base in South Boston, where she went to school: "The rum-running boats were constantly being caught and confiscated by the government and brought in by the Coast Guard. Some of these boats were battered and riddled with bullet holes from their chase with the revenue boats. It was exciting to imagine and speculate all the action of the capture, and all of us would conjure up all kinds of tales."

Silvia described the coves along the North and South Shore as providing secret places for the rumrunners to hide or unload their contraband and a place they would dump

Boston Harbor—A timeless scene. *Courtesy of Ron Goodman.*

their cargo overboard when in a close chase with the revenue boats. "Sometimes the hooch would wash up on the various island shores," Silvia wrote "and I heard that some of the Island natives would find a bottle or two of prime rum or scotch."

Silvia recounted that during the 1920s, the civilian end of Peddocks had quite a flourishing bootlegging business going. "Soldiers, it seemed, would drink anything from Listerine to rotgut. I'm not suggesting that the Peddocks Islanders sold inferior booze. I think most of it was pure, even though flavored and watered down as far as it could be and still be alcoholic."

Silvia told a number of stories about the colorful "merchants" in the booze business on the island. There was Rosie Alberts, who lived in Crab Alley (the section of Middle Head overlooking West Head on Peddocks), "cooked her lobsters and crabs outdoors on an old iron cook stove that was parked right in front of her house, and sold the shellfish and booze to wash them down."

The Goularts were another family who had a flourishing business, selling hooch in unmarked bottles, which were kept in a false wall or floor and often in the "Kazinger"— popularly known as an outhouse. Sometimes they were hidden in the ground or a woodpile—any place that would secret them from the "Revenuers."

Eddie St. John was the king of the bootleggers. He lived in a cottage with his bootlegger assistant Joe Stafford and his family. In a small cottage next door, Sunny Smith distilled the booze when the coast was clear. St. John's business came to an end when one evening Sunny Smith's still blew up, sending flames "like fireworks on the Fourth of July with shades of green, turquoise, red, yellow, and orange shooting skyward."

On December 5, 1933, the Twenty-first Amendment ended Prohibition, and with it the rum-running and bootlegging business. Most of the rum ships were sold or scrapped and their crews either went into the Merchant Marine or the U.S. Navy, which was gearing up for World War II. Surprisingly, the navy welcomed the ex-rumrunners as skilled and experienced seamen (some with "battle experience" often giving them non-commissioned officer ranks).

"A Gallops Island Man"

In 1938, when a Second World War was imminent, President Franklin Roosevelt realized that winning the war would require many ships to carry war supplies to the fronts. He ordered mass production of Liberty ships and established the U.S. Maritime Service (USMS) to train the men needed to operate these ships.

First established under the Coast Guard and later supervised by U.S. Navy officers, USMS set up basic and advanced training bases across the country. One of the advanced training bases was a radio-operator school on Gallops Island in Boston Harbor. A wartime promotional brochure said this about the Gallops Island Radio Training Station:

> To a stranger, Gallops Island, site of the United States Maritime Service Radio Training Station, is not unlike an isolated, yet pleasant mountain lake resort. Seven miles from shore and just one of many islets that dot Boston's harbor, Gallops breathes informality, but it is not long before one recognizes the effortless, yet unmistakable, poise of quiet efficiency underneath its peaceful exterior. It is an efficiency that has transformed 2,830 men from all walks of life into expertly trained Merchant Marine radio operators since Pearl Harbor.
>
> These men of Gallops Island represent something new in the history of the American Merchant Marine. They are a part—a numerically small but highly specialized part—of a planned, large-scale, intensive program involving the application of the best modern techniques of testing and classification to men of proven aptitude and then giving these men the knowledge and skills through intelligent training, to fit them for their highly important jobs at sea.
>
> Thus it is that the finely balanced training period of from twenty to thirty-two weeks makes easy the transition from dry-land sailor to sea-going man. A Gallops Island man makes this adjustment quickly. He possesses "savvy." He needs only a pair of sea legs and a few watches onboard to justify the time and money that have been spent in training him.

On September 16, 1940, President Roosevelt signed the Selective Training and Service Act into law, and along with men all around the country, the 241st Coast Artillery Regiment (Harbor Defense), Massachusetts National Guard, was ordered into active federal service. Immediately, advanced units of the 241st Coast Artillery began arriving at Fort Strong on Long Island, Fort Andrews on Peddocks Island and Fort Standish on Lovells Island. The war in Europe had begun only fifteen days before. Pearl Harbor was only fifteen months away.

Chapter 22

WORLD WAR II

With the Japanese attack on Pearl Harbor on December 7, 1941, the United States went to war against Japan and its ally, Germany—and the Boston Harbor Islands went on full alert. Garrisons were bolstered at the islands' forts, wooden piles installed and barbed wire strung out along shorelines, and sentries posted at seawalls and gun emplacements along the coast and around the islands, as rumors spread of German submarines sneaking into the harbor to shell Boston, and of a German plan to invade New England.

In just a few months after the outbreak of war, the Boston Harbor Islands were transformed into an armed archipelago. Eleven islands in the harbor—Castle, Long, Georges, Lovells, Great Brewster, Middle Brewster, Outer Brewster, Calf, Peddocks, Deer and Hog—were fortified, along with military installations set up in the coastal communities of Nahant and Winthrop on the North Shore and Hull and Scituate on the South Shore. The entrance to the harbor was heavily mined and fenced off by underwater torpedo nets. Radar-controlled coastal batteries, which could hit an enemy ship thirty miles away, were set up, and by 1943, anti-aircraft batteries, along with those at Portsmouth, New Hampshire, and Providence, Rhode Island, could blanket skies above the entire Massachusetts coast.

The Harbor Islands were training camps for recruits. As the war changed from defensive to offensive, many of the coastal artillery soldiers were sent south to train with field-artillery units and then shipped to Europe. In addition to training, each island had a specialized function. At Fort Independence, British and American scientists, working on a secret project for the U.S. Navy, set up a degaussing (the process of neutralizing the magnetic field of a ship) station on Castle Island, where a more effective mine and torpedo safety net system was built that could defend against German magnetic mines and torpedoes. (The Castle Island Degaussing Station depermed [reset or deleted the magnetism of vessels] more than five hundred Allied ships between January, 1943 and the termination of the station in November, 1945.)

On Georges Island, Fort Warren's main function during the war was to serve as the control center for the harbor's southern minefield, which included Lighthouse Channel and Nantasket Roads. If an enemy ship was sighted in their area, observers "would lock in coordinates and communicate by telephone or radio to the appropriate plotting room which then directed the huge coastal artillery guns to fire on the enemy vessels,"

Live artillery drill in 10-inch disappearing gun, Fort Warren, Georges Island, circa 1942. *Courtesy of BPL.*

wrote Jay Schmidt. "The Navy operated vessels that opened up the submarine net of the entrance to Boston Harbor to allow friendly ships to pass through. The submarine nets prevented the entry of any enemy surface torpedo boat or underwater craft." Boats operating out of Georges Island laid and maintained the mines throughout the harbor.

The northern minefield, which covered Broad Sound off of Revere and the Outer Harbor, was also heavily protected. This minefield area was electronically controlled by the Harbor Entrance Command Post at Fort Dawes on Deer Island, as well as a station on Great Brewster Island. Together, the northern and southern minefields made penetration into Boston Harbor seemingly impossible. But was it?

THE STORY OF THE U-87

Schmidt tells a story about an incident that occurred at Fort Warren one night in June 1942. Officers in the mine casement were alerted to a vessel coming near a contact mine in the minefield. A light in the mine indicator panel went on. The next day, they found that the mine was full of water and had cuts in the side similar to those made by a propeller. What caused the gash in the mine?

A naval historian discovered a report, dated June 6, 1942, documenting that a U-87 German submarine was near the Boston shipping lanes, not far from Fort Warren. The

U-boat tripped a magnetic loop detection cable, which set off signals at Point Allerton in Hull and Nahant. Did the U-87 escape before the U.S. Navy could react? The next day, there was an underwater explosion in the submarine nets near Deer Island Light. Did the U-87 blow up?

A few weeks after the explosion, a soldier on beach patrol at Fort Dawes on Deer Island found a life ring with Nazi markings that had washed up on the shore. According to a naval researcher, it was the identical type of life ring that was mounted on Type VII U-boats and possibly came from the U-87, which had been prowling near Fort Warren and Boston Light.

LIFE ON THE ISLAND

Life at Fort Warren during World War II was not much different from life during the Civil War. Men slept in the same granite-walled rooms with small coal stoves in comfortable barracks—cool in the summer since they maintained the temperature, according to Schmidt. Even training on the parade ground was similar to that activity at the fort during the Civil War. "At times I actually experienced a feeling of being on the parade ground back in 1862," wrote a soldier remembering his World War II experience at the fort.

Just as they did during the Civil War, soldiers caught fish and lobsters and dug clams to supplement army rations. The original bakery was turned into an NCO club where soldiers would play poker, dice and other games for entertainment to wile the evenings away. They also played baseball (there was an inter-island league), football and watched movies when off-duty. The U.S. Army printed a newspaper called the *Boston Harbor Defense Digest*, which was distributed to soldiers at all the harbor forts, including Fort Warren. The newspaper featured news about the war, local news and weather, and social and recreational activities on the islands.

THE CORREGIDOR OF NEW ENGLAND

The batteries of Fort Standish on Lovells and Battery Jewell on Outer Brewster made these islands among the most heavily fortified in Boston Harbor. Fort Standish had several gun batteries, guarding the main channels entering the harbor. Battery Terrill was a tunnel-accessed, concrete gun line of six-inch disappearing-gun emplacements. Battery Williams and Battery Whipple were fixed-mount gun emplacements with a concrete magazine built on a low, earthen parapet. Battery Burbeck and Battery Morris were set in deep, extensive concrete ten-inch disappearing gun pits. Together, these gun batteries faced three directions—north, east and south—covering all entrances to the harbor.

Below these batteries, reinforced concrete rooms were connected like a maze by a series of passageways. There were plotting and operations rooms; a chemical-warfare service room equipped to purify the air in case of a poison gas attack; a power room with emergency generators, heating and air-conditioning systems; storage rooms for water, fuel and ammunition; and trap doors that led to underground escape hatches. All were designed and connected to enable a person to live underground for an extended period of time.

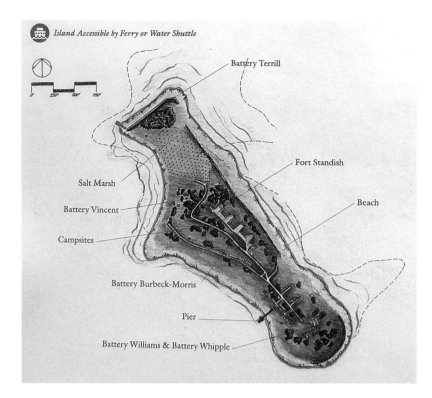

Island Accessible by Ferry or Water Shuttle

Battery Terrill

Fort Standish

Salt Marsh

Beach

Battery Vincent

Campsites

Battery Burbeck-Morris

Pier

Battery Williams & Battery Whipple

Left: Remnants of gun batteries still remain on Lovells Island. *Courtesy of NPS.*

Opposite: Diagram of Battery Jewell. *Courtesy of Gerald Butler.*

Battery Jewell, which was situated on Outer Brewster, the outermost island in the harbor, was also a completely self-sufficient installation. The battery consisted of two 6-inch radar controlled guns, operated by 125 men. Personnel were housed in three reinforced concrete barracks. The battery itself, which was bombproof and chemical-proof, was built into a man-made hill containing tunnels and ammunition storage rooms. The installation even had its own desalinization plant for fresh water supply. The army called the bunkers "The Corregidor of New England."

Even the smaller islands were pressed into military service. Gallops was the site of the U.S. Maritime Service Radar Training Station. On Hog, a tiny island off the inner shoreline of Hull in Hingham Bay, Fort Duval was fortified by two sixteen-inch guns set into a reinforced concrete tunnel to protect the guns and personnel from naval and air bombardment. On Calf Island, Theater of Operations (TO) buildings were constructed to house electrical generators, fuel, supplies and two mobile searchlights. A bantam garrison of the 241st Coast Artillery Regiment was quartered in the boathouse of the Cheney estate. There, standard army rations were supplemented with fresh fish, clams and lobster delivered in the summer months. Wild rabbits were so plentiful on Calf that the troops referred to their post as "Bugs Bunny Island."

ITALIAN POWs

Early in the war, a chemical-warfare school was setup at Fort Andrews on Peddocks Island. There, all ranks were trained in chemical warfare methods, protection and first

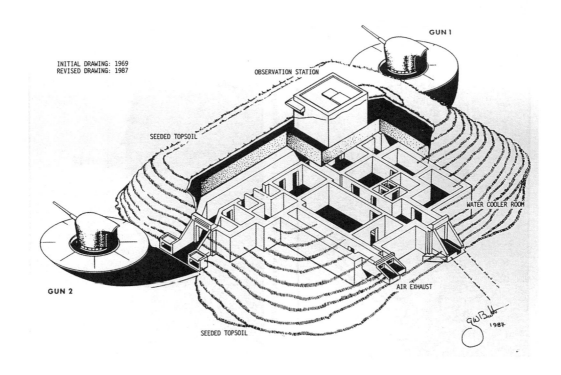

INITIAL DRAWING: 1969
REVISED DRAWING: 1987

OBSERVATION STATION

GUN 1

SEEDED TOPSOIL

WATER COOLER ROOM

GUN 2

AIR EXHAUST

SEEDED TOPSOIL

aid. As trained soldiers left Harbor Defense for overseas duty, new recruits arrived for training in the artillery methods of modern warfare. Fort Andrews was also used as a prison to hold over five hundred Italian prisoners of war during World War II.

Luigi DiGiorgio was one of those prisoners. DiGiorgio, who was a tank driver captured in North Africa in March, 1942, spent thirty months in "confinement" on Peddocks Island. A few years ago, he returned to Boston for a visit to his old prison and recounted his POW experience to the local media—an experience that was described as closer to house arrest at a nature camp than to the debilitating experience of a stalag seventeen. DiGiorgio remembered the prisoners cooking their own Italian-style food, working only five days a week and enjoying weekend visits with families in the North End (the Italian section) of Boston, even striking up romances with local girls. Women were also allowed to visit their friends on the island on weekends. "Life was beautiful," was the way DiGiorgio described his treatment at Fort Andrews.

At Fort Andrews, the lives of the POWs were inextricably linked to the American war effort. According to William Stokinger, historian at the Massachusetts Department of Conservation and Recreation (DCR), the prisoners were roused Monday through Friday mornings for an hour's sail to the Charlestown Navy Yard, where the Italians would load munitions on U.S. ships bound for the war in Europe. After eight hours in Charlestown, the work crews would be ferried back to Peddocks where the POWs would use U.S.-supplied pasta and vegetables from their own small gardens "to cook meals that even the prison commandant and his wife would join." (According to Stokinger, the

Italians held at Fort Andrews were treated differently from the German POWs confined to Fort Devens in Ayer and Fort Edwards on Cape Cod. After the Italian government abandoned its alliance with the Nazis in 1943, the Italian POWs held at Peddocks were allowed wider range of movement than other combatants.)

With the war nearly over, DiGiorgio was repatriated and went home, first to Naples and then to his village near the obliterated Nazi stronghold at Monte Cassino. Now, on his return to Peddocks nearly sixty years later, as DiGiorgio viewed the overgrown grounds and the crumbling brick buildings and collapsed wooden barracks of Fort Andrews, he remembered nostalgically how delightful life was in his two and a half years on that island.

Cold War

The harbor's coastal defenses were obsolete well before the Second World War was over, replaced first by anti-aircraft batteries and then by missiles. Deactivation of the forts had also begun before the war's end. Personnel at Fort Warren on Georges Island deactivated the harbor minefields and cleaned and stored the minefield equipment. With this mission ended, the navy saw mine defenses as obsolete and left the island. The army caretakers were also withdrawn and Georges Island was handed to the General Services Administration (GSA), which in turn offered the island to the general public in the 1950s. Other islands, such as Peddocks, Calf and Outer Brewster, met similar fates, being reduced to caretaker status and then declared surplus.

With the advent of the Korean War in June 1950, the Boston Harbor Islands once again assumed the role of defense. This time, however, it was air defense. The Cold War threat of enemy bombers attacking U.S. cities was real at that time, and the military responded to this threat by ringing important cities with anti-aircraft gun and missile batteries during the Korean War. In the 1950s, Nike-Ajax and later Nike-Hercules missile batteries were installed at twelve sites around Greater Boston. One of those sites was on Long Island, where a Nike-Ajax missile site was built, containing two underground missile storage silos with launchers and support equipment. A bridge connecting Long Island to Moon Island and the mainland, built in 1948, facilitated the movement of both hospital and military personnel and supplies to the island.

Although the Cold War persisted until nearly the end of the century, the Russians never came, and the underground silos housing the missiles were abandoned over forty years ago. For a brief time, the silos were used to provide temporary storage space for— of all things—seven hundred thousand volumes from the Boston Public Library. For the last time the curtain rang down on the role that the Boston Harbor Islands played for over three hundred years in the defense of the city, state, and nation.

Chapter 23

REMNANTS AND RENAISSANCE

After World War II, the period of neglect began in the Boston Harbor Islands. Guns of the forts were dismantled, fortifications were abandoned and the remaining installations became overgrown with thick brush and weeds. Only remnants of the islands' former military use remained.

By the 1960s, the federal government had declared Fort Independence and Castle Island surplus and deeded the property to the Commonwealth of Massachusetts. The exterior batteries were demolished and the grounds outside Fort Independence were leveled to form an urban park. On Long Island, Fort Strong's buildings were demolished with the exception of the central electric power plant, the mining casements and concrete gun emplacements. The city of Quincy proposed to buy Long Island for the 1975 World's Fair, and a proposal for a federally operated oceanographic institute was announced. Neither proposal came to fruition.

Military installations on other islands suffered a similar fate. Fort Dawes on Deer Island was abandoned, leaving the island with both an outmoded sewerage treatment plan—dumping untreated wastes into the harbor—and a deteriorating county prison. Military buildings of Fort Standish on Lovells and Fort Andrews on Peddocks were demolished, the rotting wood of their decayed and deteriorating docks and piers adding to the harbor's flotsam. On Calf, all that remains after vandals torched it was the fireplace and foundations of Julia and Arthur Cheney's estate, the *Moorings*. On the Outer Brewster, all that remains are the reinforced concrete structures and gun emplacements of Battery Jewel and prefabricated and metal buildings that long ago rusted away to the barest of frames and fragments. On Hog Island, with the guns dismantled, the battery was used as a storage facility for the town of Hull's Department of Public works, until the island was sold to a private developer, who built condominiums and changed the island's name to Spinnaker Island in the 1980s.

The greatest eyesore in the harbor was Spectacle Island. The city of Boston continued to dump raw garbage there until 1959, covering the island, filling the gullies and increasing the size of the island by nearly thirty-six acres. With deposits of trash several hundred feet deep, the dump was finally closed in 1965 when a bulldozer moving refuge on the island sank into a trash gully. Over the decades, though, the dump had produced so much methane gas that spontaneous combustion would ignite underground fires, undermining the surface of the dump, causing cave-ins and bounding the island's rocky shoreline with cliffs of decomposing trash.

The only man-made structure that remained was a ninety-foot draft chimney that loomed above the ruins of the grease-extraction plant like a ghostly smokestack of a death camp. A burning-dump odor wafted through the air surrounding the island. The final ecological insult to Spectacle was its use as a repository for a salvage firm. The unsightly debris remained on Spectacle and leached heavy metals into the harbor. The changing tides brought the island's rusted metal, broken glass and other trash to neighboring Harbor Islands and coastal areas.

Along with the abandonment of the islands was the decline of the harbor's beaches. As the automobile became widely affordable after World War II, people visited the harbor's beaches less often and the industrial character of the area discouraged many from frequenting them at all. The aversion to the harbor's beaches intensified during the polio epidemic after the war, when poor quality water was believed to transmit the debilitating disease. By the 1960s, pollution had closed many of the beaches, and by the early 1980s, the harbor was regarded, accurately or not, as the nation's "filthiest." Forty-three communities were regularly dumping inadequately treated waste into the harbor, and countless industries and ships discharged toxic pollutants that settled in sediment to form the so-called "black mayonnaise" of the harbor floor.

WATERFRONT RESURGENCE

Then gradually but steadily, a renaissance began. It started on Boston's waterfront. The city of Boston, which, like other older cities had suffered decline in the postwar decades of suburban growth, began to rebuild its historic connection to the harbor. As purely industrial uses of the waterfront declined, planning regulations began to stipulate both the presentation of "view corridors" between buildings and reducing the height of shoreline structures so as to restore a visual link to the harbor. The 1970s redevelopment of Quincy Market on Boston's waterfront, once comprised of commercial buildings in a tawdry district directly tied to waterfront businesses, began to shift the focus of the city toward the water.

In the wake of this development, hotels, restaurants, parks and walkways began to occupy formerly industrial spaces along the harbor's edge. In the 1970s, the city began work on the Harbor Walk, at that time a continuous eight-mile pedestrian walkway along the shoreline. (Today, Harbor Walk has expanded into a forty-three-mile public way—75 percent completed—that stretches around Boston Harbor from Milton in the south to Revere in the north.) With the growing appeal of harbor tours and several passenger ferry companies competing to conduct these tours, the focus shifted to the Boston Harbor Islands.

A number of master plans for the redevelopment of the Harbor Islands were proposed, the first since Olmsted proposed the reforestation of the islands in 1886. These plans viewed the Harbor Islands as the key component of the ecosystems and the natural and cultural history of the harbor. Some envisioned the islands as an "emerald tiara" that complemented the extensive "emerald necklace" that Olmstead and Eliot created for the Boston Metropolitan area in the 1890s.

Boston skyline, inner harbor. *Courtesy of MWRA.*

Amidst this growing sentiment, the Commonwealth of Massachusetts passed landmark legislation in 1970 that authorized public ownership of the Boston Harbor Islands to enhance in perpetuity public recreation and preserve open space. The legislation, in effect, created the Boston Harbor Islands State Park. Soon after the legislation was passed, the commonwealth purchased Peddocks Island from private owners; and Georges and Lovells Islands from the U.S. government. The city of Boston acquired Castle Island, placing it under the jurisdiction of the Metropolitan District Commission (MDC), a state agency.

In the 1980s, the commonwealth purchased more islands, mostly from the federal government. Among them: Bumpkin, Calf, Little Calf, Gallops, Grape, Greater Brewster, Middle Brewster, Outer Brewster, Green, Hangman's, Raccoon, Sheep, and Slate Islands, placing them under the State Department of Environmental Management (DEM). DEM and the City of Boston jointly owned Spectacle Island; and a third agency, the Massachusetts Water Resources Authority (MWRA), created by the commonwealth in 1986 to provide water to metropolitan Boston and abate wastewater discharge into Boston Harbor, owned Deer and Nut Islands. Collectively, these islands defined the outlines of the new state park.

Two mega-projects, though, contributed more than any other factor to the public's discovery of Boston's maritime past and the recreational potential of the Boston Harbor Islands.

The Big Dig, officially called the Central Artery/Tunnel Project, was the largest public-works project ever undertaken in this country. Started in 1991, it was 94 percent completed by the summer of 2004, with final completion by 2006, at a cost of nearly $15 billion. (It is still not finished.) The Big Dig is likened to a triple-bypass heart surgery, cutting the heart of Boston open and unclogging the city's blocked arteries. In its first phase, the project called for tearing down the old elevated highway over downtown Boston and constructing a third tunnel, the Ted Williams Tunnel, named after the famed Boston Red Sox slugger, running from South Boston to Logan International Airport. In its final form, the Big Dig is comprised of nearly 43 miles of underground superhighway and over 160 lane miles of superhighway in tunnels, bridges, viaducts and surface roads. The southernmost tip runs from Roxbury and South Boston to the northernmost tip of Charlestown, the North End and East Boston. Even before the Big Dig was completed, the demolition of the elevated highway brought down the barriers to the harbor, and opened up and connected Boston's access to the waterfront and the Harbor Islands beyond.

The other mega-project was the Boston Harbor Project. Under the direction of the Massachusetts Water Resources Authority (MWRA), the Boston Harbor Project was started in 1986 and became fully operational by the year 2000. The project cost $4.2 billion, the largest public works undertaking in the country until The Big Dig. It included the construction of a new secondary wastewater-treatment plant on Deer Island to replace the failing and undersized primary treatment plants on Deer and Nut Islands; a tunnel from Nut Island to the Deer Island Treatment Plant (DITP) for secondary treatment and an outfall-diffuser system to discharge treated effluent nine and a half miles offshore into Massachusetts Bay, increasing dilution and minimizing potential environmental impacts in the bay.

The effects of the cleanup of Boston Harbor's water quality were dramatic. Harbor water quality became cleaner than it had been for decades. While former treatment plants failed to meet water quality standards in the past, now under the new DITP, bacteria levels are greatly reduced and water quality vastly improved. Fishing for blue fish, striped bass, cod and flounder improved significantly, and water quality at the harbor beaches is cleaner. In 1987, there were sixty beach closings due to high bacteria levels in the harbor. By 1993, there were only nineteen closings. As one official put it some years later, "if there were no Boston Harbor Project, there would be no Boston Harbor Islands National Park."

The Making of the Boston Harbor Islands National Park Area

In his book, *Participatory Ecological Governance: Insights from a Case Study of the Boston Harbor Islands Partnership*, Rob Moir, marine environmentalist, wrote that at the peak of Boston's economic prosperity and ecological initiatives, the best possible political conditions for creating a national park came together. Congressman Gerry Studds announced that after many years of public service he would step down from office at the end of 1996. His district included the southern portions of Boston Harbor. In a meeting with Terry Savage then superintendent of the Boston Support Office of the National Park Service, the idea for a new national park came up, and Studds liked it, later admitting "In all

Ships of sail cruise Boston Harbor. *Courtesy of Ron Goodman.*

my embarrassingly long number of years in public life, I never came upon an idea with more support. It is the most obvious and wonderful of ideas."

Congress has a policy of honoring a departing senior representative's last legislative wish. Studds chose the creation of a national park in the Boston Harbor Islands as his legacy. The political capital generated in creating a national park in an urban setting, in which seven million citizens lived within a fifty-mile radius, was enormous. With that in mind, in 1995, Congressmen Studds (Democrat) and Peter Torkildsen (Republican), whose district included the coastal cities of Lynn and Salem, in a rare bipartisan effort, introduced legislation in the U.S. House of Representatives for the creation of a Boston Harbor Islands National Park. Joseph Moakley, first as a state senator and then as a U.S. Congressman from Boston, was also instrumental in building support for a national park in Boston Harbor.

On the senatorial side, Massachusetts senators Edward Kennedy and John Kerry introduced companion legislation in the U.S. Senate. It was clear, though, that both of the senators understood the mood of the majority Republican-controlled Senate—the government was already too big, and the National Park Service already managed too many parks at too great expense to American taxpayers. At the same time, Democrats were speaking of increasing government efficiency without adding levels of government, while calling for more citizen participation in government decision-making.

Gauging the mood in the Senate, Kerry, with Kennedy's support, introduced a bill that had a better chance of getting passed in Congress than one calling for the establishment of a new federally owned national park. Kerry's bill called for establishing a unique partnership among the federal, state and local governments and the private sector and requiring at least 75 percent of the operational expenses for the park coming from non-federal funding. In other words, a national park would be established where the federal government did not have to buy property and could only be requested—but not obligated—to pay for at most a quarter of the operating expenses on an annual basis. This was a new concept of park governance—a unique partnership—composed of federal, state and municipal government; private sector organizations; and interest groups, including Native Americans—all on equal footing. Was it possible that these diverse groups could work together? (That is a question that can still be asked today.)

From its inception, legislation creating a Boston Harbor Islands National Park did not go unchallenged. National Park Service (NPS) nomenclature requires that a national park contain significant natural beauty of unspoiled and pristine areas along with "large land or water areas to help provide adequate protection of the resources." The Boston Harbor Islands, located in a largely populated and altered landscape could not meet these requirements.

The designation "National Recreation Area," however, is one that the NPS uses for areas that are managed under cooperative agreements with at least one other federal agency. Examples of national recreation areas (NRA) are Gateway NRA in New York Harbor, with areas in New Jersey; and Golden Gate NRA in the San Francisco Bay area. Even though the Boston Harbor Islands are less than one-tenth the size of either New York or San Francisco's NRA, park supporters believed the best chance for the Boston Harbor Islands to become a unit of the National Park System was if they were designated a "National Recreation Area."

Native Americans, however, were furious with the designation of "Recreation Area," finding it offensive and disrespectful of "the thousands of Native Americans who had been incarcerated by colonists on the Boston Harbor Islands in the seventeenth and eighteenth century." Many were sent to the Harbor Islands, particularly Deer Island, during and after King Philip's War and, while incarcerated, were given little food, water or shelter—few survived. Not only were Native Americans who fought against the colonists sent there, but also those who fought alongside the colonists. Even Native Americans who had converted to Christianity and lived with the colonists as "praying Indians" were sent to the island detention camps. Today, more than fifteen tribes (federally and non-federally recognized), including the Delaware, Narragansett, Neponset, Wampanoag, Nipmuck, Natick, Penobscot, Pequot and Mohican, to name a number of them, claim connections to the Boston Harbor Islands because ancestors of their tribes were imprisoned there.

Native Americans testified before the Senate that to call the burial grounds resulting from "the Massachusetts Colony's government policy of passive extermination" a national recreation area was unacceptable. "It would be like letting people dance on our graves," testified one Native American. Park advisors agreed that on an "as known as" name, the park would not include the word "recreation." Instead, it was agreed on that the "Boston Harbor Islands, A National Park Area" would be the wording on the park's stationery, website and signage.

Harbor Islands ferry terminal on Long Wharf. *Courtesy of Ron Goodman.*

At the eleventh hour, another challenge to legislation creating a Boston Harbor Islands national park suddenly emerged—Castle Island wanted out. Connected to South Boston by an artificial isthmus of landfill, Castle Island is the closest harbor "island" to downtown Boston and it would have been the most accessible property in the national park. Castle Island and Fort Independence were then managed by the Metropolitan District Commission (MDC) with the Castle Island Association, a close-knit South Boston community organization, which did not want to be included in a federally run national park. Park proponents could not sway the Castle Island Association, which was supported by their many friends in South Boston, state government and the MDC, to come aboard. It was a big loss and may have set a precedent that will raise the question of community and land secession from the new park in the future.

Nonetheless, Castle Island has been designated a historical landmark, and its historical and geographical connection to the Boston Harbor Islands does give, to some extent, a sense that it is part and parcel of the national park.

The Omnibus Parks and Public Lands Management Act of 1996 became law during the final hours of the 104th Congress in October 1996. Section 1024 of the law established the thirty-four islands and peninsulas in Boston Harbor as a new park within the National Park Service. The NPS acquired no land in the park, nor was there any funding committed to the new park. Funding would be decided later based in what the non-federal partners would contribute for their three-to-one portion of the match.

The law established the Boston Harbor Islands Partnership, a twelve-member body consisting of federal, state and local authorities and the private sector, and gave it the task of developing and implementing a general plan for the Boston Harbor Islands. The partnership's twelve members included the National Park Service; U.S. Coast Guard; Massachusetts Department of Environmental Management (DEM); MDC (the latter two now part of the Massachusetts Department of Recreation); Massachusetts Port Authority; Massachusetts Water Resources Authority (MWRA); City of Boston Office of Environmental Services; Boston Redevelopment Authority; Trustees of Reservations; Thompson Island Outward Bound Education Center; Boston Harbor Islands Alliance, a nonprofit organization whose purpose is to provide financial support; and two members from an advisory council, whose role is to advise the partnership in the planning and operation of the park through public involvement.

As the legislation states, the mission of the Boston Harbor Islands National Park Area is "to preserve and protect a drumlin island system within Boston Harbor, along with is natural, cultural and historic resources; to tell the islands' individual stories and enhance public understanding and appreciation of the island system as a whole; and to provide public access to the islands and surrounding waters for the education, enjoyment, and scientific and scholarly research of this and future generations."

To manage this unique model, the Boston Harbor Islands National Park Area involves innovative approaches to consensus-building, environmental leadership and "participatory ecological governance," a process involving public groups in decision-making on environmental and natural resource matters. The twenty-first century would test the viability of this model of ecological governance for the Boston Harbor Islands.

Chapter 24

THE TWENTY-FIRST CENTURY

In 2000, under enabling legislation for the Boston Harbor Islands National Park Area, the partnership completed a draft of the General Management Plan. The plan is a broad-based document laying out a twenty-year prospectus for resource protection, research and information, visitor access and enjoyment, education and interpretation, management and operations and external cooperation.

The plan calls for dividing the Harbor Islands Park into management zones to help balance between resource preservation and visitor use in each part of the park. For example, island zones selected for historic preservation include the forts on Georges, Lovells, and Peddocks Islands; also the lighthouses on Little Brewster, the Graves and Long Island. Island zones selected for their natural features, predominantly reflecting forces of nature and retaining some feeling of "wilderness" include all of the Brewsters (except Little Brewster where Boston Light is located) and the Graves. Zones with management emphasis on visitor services and park facilities offering opportunities for recreational, cultural and educational activities include Georges, Lovells, Peddocks and Spectacle Islands, where ferry piers and supporting facilities are located.

One of the long-range goals, essential to the water-based infrastructure of the park, calls for the development of gateways—mainland ferry departure points—"to provide windows to the islands and their manifold activities and resources." The purpose of the gateways is "to attract, welcome and educate national park visitors and create excitement about the excursion that lies ahead." Long Wharf, Fan Pier in Boston Harbor and Hewitt's Cove in Hingham Harbor are among the larger, more active gateway proposals.

Another long-range goal is to develop the various islands for unique environmental experiences. Peddocks Island, one of the largest and most ecologically diverse of the Boston Harbor Islands, was chosen as the flagship project. The plan calls for establishing the Peddocks Island EcoRetreat and Family Camp as an all-inclusive destination in the harbor, offering rustic tents and cabins, central dining and meeting rooms in restored historic buildings and featuring environmental education and recreational activities. The island's many attractions would include the themes of Native American culture, military history, environmental studies and a range of science and technology courses.

Gateways and eco-retreats are still off in the future, however. For the present, the national park has more immediate and pressing needs. First off, the national park was conceived

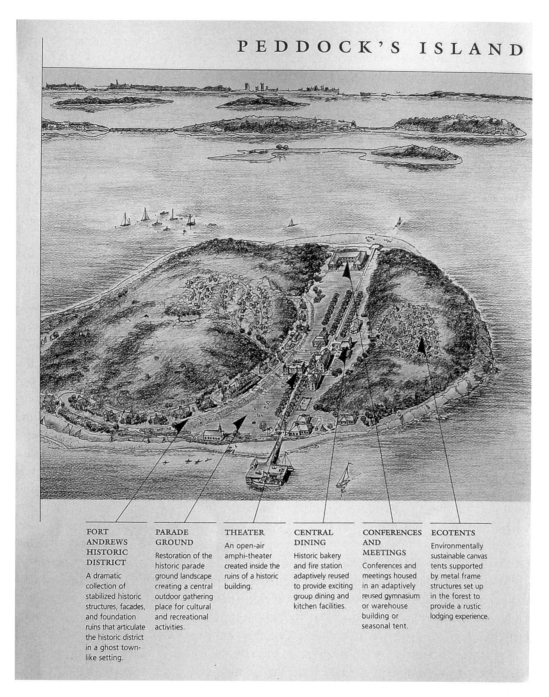

PEDDOCK'S ISLAND

FORT ANDREWS HISTORIC DISTRICT	PARADE GROUND	THEATER	CENTRAL DINING	CONFERENCES AND MEETINGS	ECOTENTS
A dramatic collection of stabilized historic structures, facades, and foundation ruins that articulate the historic district in a ghost town-like setting.	Restoration of the historic parade ground landscape creating a central outdoor gathering place for cultural and recreational activities.	An open-air amphi-theater created inside the ruins of a historic building.	Historic bakery and fire station adaptively reused to provide exciting group dining and kitchen facilities.	Conferences and meetings housed in an adaptively reused gymnasium or warehouse building or seasonal tent.	Environmentally sustainable canvas tents supported by metal frame structures set up in the forest to provide a rustic lodging experience.

Artist's conception of Peddocks Island EcoRetreat. *Courtesy of NPS.*

in a different era. The events of 9/11 changed everything. Security in Boston Harbor became the major issue; recreation was secondary. As in other ports, the U.S. Coast Guard heightened security in the harbor, placing more restrictions on port traffic and recreational boating and sailing, especially in the light of the vulnerability to a terrorist attack on a liquefied natural gas (LNG) facility in Everett on Boston's inner harbor.

In addition to these new restrictions, the national park faces a host of other challenges. Foremost among them are resource stabilization and reclamation. Forty-seven historical buildings and fortifications on the islands are in the state of collapse. Little money has been available for stabilizing and securing these sites. (Some, like Fort Andrews on Peddocks Island, may be beyond repair and will have to be demolished.) In addition, several archaeological sites are threatened by continual erosion and nearly $1 million is needed to stabilize coastal banks where the sites are located.

Even costlier and more difficult are the remediation actions needed to clean up the environmental hazards on eight islands. Contamination from underground storage tanks (UST), asbestos, coal and lead found in many World War II structures has required an arduous and costly cleanup process. Asbestos has been removed from Fort Andrews's buildings on Peddocks and from buildings on Outer and Great Brewster Islands, along with UST removals, and Long Island, along with hydraulic oil from the former Nike Missile silo. Although a total of nine tons of asbestos was removed from Gallops, the island remains closed. Finishing Gallops's cleanup is estimated to cost $8 million, a tab that the Park Service hopes the U.S. Army Corps of Engineers will pick up.

In the early years of the new century, things looked bleak for the national park. Efforts to build parks on the harbor islands were mired in disagreements between public agencies and political squabbles over development plans. Operating the park was no easy task either. Georges Island operated for a few years without running water; it needed a new system and fuel oil contamination on the island had to be cleaned up. Docks on Great Brewster, Lovells and Peddocks continually needed repair. Public moorings that were anchored off the islands were stolen and had to be replaced. Estimates to install basic utilities on Peddocks came in at a staggering $3.8 million. (Utilities were later installed on Peddocks through a $5 million "mitigation" grant from Duke Energy Company.)

Water transportation continued to be a major issue, with ferry communications, scheduling, capacity, equipment failures and rising fuel prices driving ticket prices higher, undermining a critical component of the national park. At one point, so many islands were either closed, partially closed or delayed in opening due to hazardous wastes and maintenance problems, ferry scheduling difficulties or inadequate funding that one official was prompted to refer to the park "as the incredible shrinking islands." Then the fortunes of the park appeared to have turned around.

SPECTACLE ISLAND

In 2006, after twelve years in development and six years of bureaucratic delays, Spectacle Island was finally opened to the public. During this period, Spectacle had undergone an extreme makeover from a 97-acre "sacrifice zone" in the middle of Boston Harbor, as one contemporary writer put it, "a place where old horses once were processed into glue

Spectacle Island Pier. *Courtesy of Ron Goodman.*

and where politicians perennially dreamed of putting unwanted facilities such as sludge dumps and incinerators," to the 120-acre "emerald gateway" to the Boston Harbor Islands—fifteen minutes from downtown Boston.

Back in the 1990s, Big Dig authorities were looking for a site to dump the dirt excavated from the Ted Williams Tunnel and other work sites. City and state officials agreed that excavated materials could be dumped on Spectacle in return for the Big Dig building a park on the island. Big Dig workers hauled 3.7 million cubic yards of dirt, gravel and clay from the mainland, using the excavated materials to landscape and refurbish the island. Today, at a cost of $200 million, paid for by the Big Dig, Spectacle's two drumlins have increased in height—the North Drumlin from 95 feet to 155 feet, now the highest natural point in the harbor, and the South Drumlin, 65 feet to 125 feet. Thousands of trees and shrubs were planted over the island; five miles of trails, two sandy beaches, a thirty-six-slip marina and a $5-million visitors' center constructed. Plans for Spectacle include "zero-emission power" with electricity generated by solar power and experimental electric cars and bikes put to use on its pathways.

THE PARK UNDER ATTACK

About the same time the opening of Spectacle Island was announced, a proposal suddenly emerged that threatened to rip the national park to pieces. AES Corp., a giant

Arlington, Virginia-based energy company, proposed purchasing Outer Brewster Island in Boston Harbor and building a $500 million liquefied natural gas (LNG) facility on the island.

AES warned that natural gas supply was growing only 2 percent in New England, while consumption was growing 5 percent. Massachusetts, along with other New England states, was heading toward a gas crisis, unless a new source of natural gas supply was found for the region. The company saw Outer Brewster, a remote twenty-acre, treeless island lying far out in the harbor, eight miles from Boston, as a very favorable site to locate a LNG facility. The company said that Outer Brewster meets all the criteria for establishing a LNG storage terminal.

The island is surrounded by water depths of at least fifty feet needed to allow vessels access at all tides; and by an "exclusion zone" to protect neighboring communities in the event of a pool fire or flammable vapor cloud. It is within three miles of an existing gas pipeline and remote enough with no population within the one-mile thermal impact zone. AES added in its proposal that having tankers offload the LNG eight miles from downtown Boston would be far safer than having LNG tankers entering into the inner harbor where the Distrigas terminal in Everett is located, the only other LNG facility in Massachusetts.

The AES proposal was like a bombshell, catching everyone by surprise. The idea of taking the island from a national park and converting it into a site for a LNG facility seemed preposterous and unlawful. But was it?

Although Outer Brewster is part of the Boston Harbor Islands National Park Area, the island is owned by the commonwealth of Massachusetts and, therefore, the state could sell it. Backed by a local public-relations firm and a legion of high-powered Beacon Hill lobbyists, AES pushed its proposal onto a fast track for a legislative hearing. The timing of the proposal appeared quite advantageous. Facing skyrocketing gas prices and gas shortages on the horizon, even a possibility of brownouts in the coming winter, lawmakers were anxious to find a site for a LNG facility. Proposals for LNG facilities in Fall River and Gloucester were meeting resistance. The Outer Brewster, which AES described as a "barren wasteland" that discouraged visitors, with no recreational facilities like trails, piers or docks, remote from any population area, would be very suitable for a LNG site. In its publicity campaign, the company's public-relations firm denigrated the Outer Brewster, highlighting the "barren wasteland" aspects of the island, showing pictures of graffiti on the remnants of the island's World War II gun batteries and barracks and the litter and debris in an abandoned quarry.

A consultant was hired to help establish a group of citizens who publicly supported the AES proposal and, based on a study that showed the island location could reduce the number of tanker trips to Everett, suggested it could replace that terminal. In fact, in a letter sent to the legislature and obtained by the *Boston Globe*, the company said its proposal would offer an alternative to letting tankers into the harbor during times of a terrorist threat. The terrorism message was echoed in LNG advocate flyers and websites "warning that ships headed to the Everett facility are floating bombs that steam past thousands of homes and 500,000 residents who are in constant danger."

In summary, the AES message to legislators: "Our proposal offers a necessary new source of natural gas supply while providing maximum public safety and significant revenues to the state and local government." For a ninety-nine-year lease on Outer Brewster Island, AES would pay the state $10 million annually and about $5 million in taxes annually.

The proposal quickly gained legislative support. "I think it's a sound proposal that has a lot of merit," said one state legislator. "It's the only LNG proposal on the table that will give state governance control over the siting process, plus provide a safe and secure method of delivering much-needed energy supply to the region," said another legislator. Other state lawmakers, as well as the governor, began to speak out on the potential merit of a LNG facility on the Outer Brewster and that it warranted further review.

Seeing the AES juggernaut powering the proposal through the legislature, two dozen environmental and marine interest groups joined together in a coalition to fight the bill. Led by Save the Harbor/Save the Bay, the Save the Brewsters coalition included some of the state's major environmental advocates, such as the Conservation Law Foundation, Environmental League of Massachusetts, Friends of the Boston Harbor Islands, Hull Lifesaving Museum, Island Alliance and the Massachusetts chapters of the Audubon Society and the Sierra Club. Under aggressive and tireless leadership, the coalition organized a campaign to battle the proposal. A phone and letter-writing campaign to legislators and the media was undertaken, expressing opposition to the proposal; public forums were held, discussing the issue; and off a major highway on the South Shore, a bill board was erected, carrying the anti-LNG message: "The Harbor Islands Are Not For Sale."

To AES's challenge that the Outer Brewster is desolate and unvisited, of little value to anyone, littered with abandoned WWII buildings, and should be put to better use, the Save the Brewsters coalition answered in an open letter carried by the media:

> *Outer Brewster is in a national park. It is part of the archipelago of the harbor's outermost islands. Together with its surrounding islands—Calf, Green, Middle Brewster, Great Brewster, and Little Brewster (home of Boston Light)—Outer Brewster's waters include pristine Calf Bay and Brewster Cove. The island is home to many species of land and shore birds; its waters are home to abundant waterfowl, fish species, important lobster beds and the only seal colony in Boston Harbor. Though rugged in appearance, the island is actually part of a fragile and unique ecosystem in Boston Harbor, which citizens invested $4.5 billion to clean up, and is the very reason the harbor and islands were declared a national park ten years ago.*
>
> *Hundreds of fishermen and lobstermen fish recreationally and commercially from the waters off Outer Brewster Island. Annually, thousands of recreational boaters enjoy unfettered access to the waterways entering and leaving Boston Harbor, all passing adjacent to Outer Brewster. The region's kayaking community, its rowers, scuba-divers and other small-boaters are drawn to Outer Brewster for the cleanest undersea waters in the region, as well as its unspoiled wilderness and unparalleled historic and natural vistas. The island's abundant life reveals the healthy cycles of species' renewal fostered in teeming*

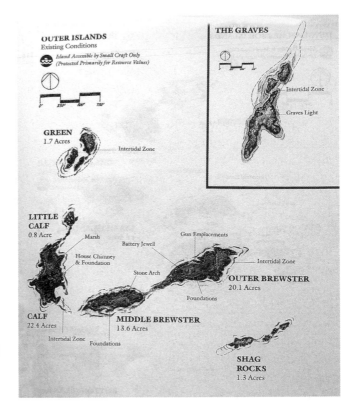

OUTER ISLANDS
Existing Conditions

Island Accessible by Small Craft Only
(Protected Primarily for Resource Values)

0 250' 500' 750'

GREEN
1.7 Acres — Intertidal Zone

THE GRAVES

Intertidal Zone

Graves Light

LITTLE CALF
0.8 Acre

Marsh

House Chimney & Foundation

Battery Jewell

Gun Emplacements

Stone Arch

Intertidal Zone

OUTER BREWSTER
20.1 Acres

Foundations

CALF
22.4 Acres

Intertidal Zone Foundations

MIDDLE BREWSTER
13.6 Acres

SHAG ROCKS
1.3 Acres

Right: Outer Islands, proposal to locate LNG facility on Outer Brewster. *Courtesy of NPS.*

Below: View of Boston skyline and Deer Island Sewage Treatment Plant from the Outer Islands. *Courtesy of Ron Goodman.*

Sails in the sunset. *Courtesy of Ron Goodman.*

waters and undisturbed landscapes, all of which directly and positively impact the health of the national park's entire natural system.

Construction of the proposed terminal would guarantee the irreversible destruction of vital fish and lobster nurseries, disruption of critical bird and butterfly migratory routes, would close historic and thriving fishing grounds and boating routes and would ban visitors from the island. Outer Brewster's highest elevation is sixty feet. LNG storage tanks drilled deep into the island's bedrock would still stand thirty feet above the island's profile. The LNG tankers will tower an additional hundred feet above the island's surface (nearly twice the height of neighboring Boston Light). These tankers and their terminal will not sit quietly, but will create substantial undersea and over-water noise, discharge large volumes of bilge and other wastewater, and continuously burn shrill lights that will obscure Boston Light and the night sky, while dominating the coastline. What is now a spectacular vista that quiets the mind and excites the imagination will become an industrial eyesore—forever.

Despite the growing opposition to the proposal, AES powerbrokers on Beacon Hill managed to get the House Rules Committee to suspend the rules, permitting AES's late-filed bill to be admitted to the House in November 2005.Before a packed legislative hearing room in the State House the following March, a joint committee heard testimonies for and against House Bill 4500, authorizing the leasing of Outer Brewster Island in Boston Harbor for the purpose of siting a LNG facility on the island.

Proponents of the bill pointed out that the Outer Brewster site would combine the advantages of a mainland facility and the enhanced safety features of an offshore facility. They also pointed out that large amounts of LNG could be safely stored at this facility and would pose no threat to residents, the closest facility lying beyond the federally mandated safety zone. And that it is "one step in meeting the expanding energy needs of the citizens of the commonwealth in a safe and environmentally responsible manner."

Capping off the testimonies of the opponents of the bill, Bruce Jacobson, the superintendent of the Boston Harbor Islands National Park Area, in citing the Boston Harbor Islands as a unit of the national park system, said "the fundamental purpose of all units of the national park system is to conserve the scenery and the natural and historic objects and the wildlife, therein, and to provide for the enjoyment of the same in such manner and by such means as will leave them unimpaired for the enjoyment of future generations."

The committee voted to send the proposal to a study committee—a step that effectively derailed the proposal. The Boston Harbor Islands National Park was saved. It was a victory for park advocates—this time. Both environmentalists and lawmakers, however, expect the measure to resurface in some form; and AES has vowed to press on with its proposal. A battle was won, but there would be more wars to be fought in the years ahead.

From the perspective of the early twenty-first century, the Outer Brewster LNG episode serves as a cautionary tale: The Boston Harbor Islands National Park is a fragile ecosystem, vulnerable to so many forces; its governance is still wanting in so many areas. The park's preservation as an urban wilderness, perhaps its very survival, will demand constant vigilance and steadfast action by its supporters in the coming decades of the twenty-first century.

BIBLIOGRAPHY

BOOKS

Athearn, Robert G., and editors. *American Heritage New Illustrated History of the United States.* 16 vols. New York: Fawcett Publications, Inc., 1971.

Baker, William A. *The Boston Marine Society in the American War for Independence.* Boston: Boston Marine Society, 1976.

Bunting, William. *Portrait of the Port of Boston, 1852–1914.* Cambridge, MA: The Belknap Press of Harvard University Press, 1994.

Butler, Gerald W. *The Guns of Boston Harbor.* Nahant, MA: 1ˢᵗ Books, 1999.

———. *Images of America: The Military History of Boston's Harbor Islands.* Charleston, SC: Arcadia Publishing, 2000

Cobb, David, and Alex Krieger, eds. *Mapping Boston.* Cambridge, MA: The MIT Press, 1999.

Committee for the Preservation of Hull's History. *Images of America: Hull and Nantasket Beach.* Charleston, SC: Arcadia Publishing, 1999.

Crosby, Irving. *Boston Through the Ages, The Geological Story of Greater Boston.* Cambridge, MA: The Murray Printing Company, 1928.

Dolin, Eric Jay. *Political Waters: The Long, Dirty, Contentious, Incredibly Expensive But Eventually Triumphant History of Boston Harbor.* Amherst and Boston: University of Massachusetts Press, 2004.

Dow, George Frances and John Henry Edmonds. *The Pirates of the New England Coast 1630–1730.* New York: Dover Publications, Inc., 1996.

Ellis, Joseph J. *His Excellency, George Washington.* New York: Knopf, 2004.

Emilio, Luis F. *History of the Fifty-Forth Regiment Volunteer Infantry 1863–1865.* Boston: The Boston Book Company, 1894.

Fowler, William M., Jr. *Boston Looks Seaward: The Story of the Port, 1630–1940.* Boston: Northeastern University Press, 1985.

———. *Jack Tars and Commodores: The American Navy 1783–1815.* Boston: Houghton Mifflin, 1984

———. *Rebels Under Sail: The American Navy During the Revolution.* New York: Charles Scribner's & Sons, 1976.

Handlin, Oscar. *Boston's Immigrants 1790–1880.* Cambridge, MA: The Belknap Press of Harvard University Press, 1969.

Howe, Henry F. *Prologue to New England. The Forgotten Century of the Explorers.* New York: Farrar & Rinehart, Inc. 1943.

Kales, David, and Emily Kales. *All About the Boston Harbor Islands.* Hingham, MA: Hewitts Cove Publishing, 1993 (Revised Edition).

Kolata, Gina. *The Story of the Great Influenza Pandemic of 1918 and the Search for the Virus that Caused It.* New York: Farrar, Straus & Giroux, 1999.

Lepore, Jill. *The Name of War: King Philip's War and the Origins of American Identity.* New York: Alfred A. Knopf, 1998.

Mandell, Daniel R. *Frontier Indians: Behind the Frontier Indians in Eighteenth Century Eastern Massachusetts.* Lincoln, Nebraska: University of Nebraska Press, 1996.

McCullough, David. *1776.* New York: Simon & Schuster, 2005.

Metcalf, Leonard, and Harrison P. Eddy. *American Sewerage Practices.* Vol. I. New York: McGraw-Hill Book Company, 1914.

Moir, Rob. *Participatory Ecological Governance: Insights from a Case Study of the Boston Harbor Islands Partnership.* PhD. thesis in Environmental Studies at Antioch New England Graduate School, Keene, NH, 2002.

Morison, Samuel Eliot. *Maritime History of Massachusetts 1783–1860.* Boston: Northeastern University Press, 1980.

Nash, Roderick. *Wilderness and the American Mind*. New Haven, CT: Yale University Press, 1987.

O'Connor, Thomas H. *Civil War Boston. Homefront and Battlefield*. Boston: Northeastern University Press, 1997.

Quinlin, Michael P. *Irish Boston*. Guilford, CT: The Globe Pequot Press, 2004.

Reid, William J. *Castle Island and Fort Independence*. Boston: Trustees of the Public Library of the City of Boston, 1995.

Roberts, Nancy. *Blackbeard and Other Pirates of the Atlantic Coast*. Winston-Salem, NC: John F. Blair Publishing, 1993.

Russell, Howard S. *Indian New England Before the Mayflower*. Hanover, NH: University Press of New England, 1980.

Schmidt, Jay. *Fort Warren: New England's Most Historic Civil War Site*. Amherst, NH: UBT Press, 2003.

Silvia, Matilda. *Once Upon an Island*. Cohasett, MA: Hot House Press, 2003.

Snow, Edward Rowe. *Amazing Sea Stories Never Told Before*. New York: Dodd, Mead and Company, 1957

———. *The Islands of Boston Harbor*. New York: Dodd, Mead & Co., 1971.

———. *The Lighthouses of New England, 1716–1973*. New York: Dodd, Mead & Co., 1973.

Sweetser, M.F. *King's Handbook of Boston Harbor*. Cambridge, MA: Moses King Publisher, 1882.

Sullivan, Robert F. *Shipwrecks and Nautical Lore of Boston Harbor*. Chester, CT: The Globe Pequot Press, 1990.

Todd, Lewis, and Merle Curti. *The Rise of the American Nation*. New York: Harcourt Brace Jovanovich, Publishers, 1982.

Walker, H.C., and Willard Brewer Walker. *A History of World's End*. Milton, MA: The Trustees of Reservations, 1973.

Whitehill, Walter Muir. *Boston: A Topographical History.* Cambridge, MA: The Belnap Press of Harvard University Press, 1968 (second edition enlarged).

Woodham-Smith, Cecil. *The Great Hunger: Ireland 1845–1849.* New York: Penguin Putnam Inc., 1962.

REPORTS

Boston Harbor Islands Advisory Council. *Analysis of the Boston Harbor Islands National Park Area Five-year Strategic Plan*, March, 2006.

Boston Harbor Islands Partnership. *Realizing the Promise. Economic Sustainability Strategy for the Boston Harbor Islands National Park Area.* 2001 www.bostonislands.com.

Carella, Elizabeth. *Rainsford Island. Archeological Reconnaissance and Management Plan.* Boston Landscape Commission and Massachusetts Historical Commission, October 2002.

City of Boston. *History of Boston's Harbor Islands—Long Island.* http://www.cityofBoston.gov/environment/harbor_islands_history.asp.17. April 2002.

Foley, Mary K. *Significant Natural Resources of the Brewster Island Cluster: Boston Harbor Islands National Park Area.* Technical Report NPS/NER/NRTR-2005 F/024. National Park Service, Northeast Region. Boston, MA. October 2005.

Jacobson, Bruce, and Judith Pederson, eds. Proceedings of a Seminar—*Boston Harbor Islands National Park Area, 2002 Islands Biodiversity.* Cambridge, MA: Massachusetts Institute of Technology, MIT Sea Grant Program, May, 2002.

King, Marsha. *Historic Document Report: An Historic Cemetery Site at Deer Island House of Corrections.* Prepared for the Massachusetts Water Resources Authority by the Public Archeology Laboratory, 1992.

Kuhl, Ellen. *The Cemeteries of the Boston Almshouse and Hospital.* Environmental Department of the City of Boston, 2003.

Luedtke, Barbara. E. *The Archeology of Thompson Island.* Department of Anthropology, University of Massachusetts, Boston, 1996.

Massachusetts Department of Environmental Management. *Boston Harbor Islands State Park 1986 Master Plan.*

BIBLIOGRAPHY

Massachusetts Water Resources Authority. *Beyond the Boston Harbor Project. The State of Boston Harbor, 1997–1998.* Technical Report No. 00-05. Boston, MA. 2000.

———. *Deer Island House of Correction, Massachusetts.* MWRA Section 106. Documentation Habs No.MA-1251. Prepared by McGinley Hart & Associates, Architects and Preservation Planners for Tsoi/Kobus & Associates, Architects, March, 1991.

———. *5 Year Progress Report 1995–1999.* www.mwra.com. 2002

———. *The State of Boston Harbor. Mapping the Harbor's Recovery,* 2002. Technical Report No. 2002-09.

Metropolitan Area Planning Council. *Boston Harbor Islands Comprehensive Plan.* Boston, MA. 1972.

———. *Open Space and Recreation Program for Metropolitan Boston.* Vol.2. Boston, MA. 1968

Metropolitan District Commission and the Fort Revere Park Preservation Society, Hull, MA. *Telegraph Hill-Early History.*

National Park Service. *Cultural Landscape Report for the Boston Harbor Islands. History, Resources and Recommendations,* History of the Islands. Vol.1. (Draft) Olmsted Center for Landscape Preservation, Boston, MA.

———. North Atlantic Region. *Boston Harbor Islands, Report of a Special Resource Study,* 1994.

———. Northeast Region. *Boston Harbor Islands, A National Park Area. General Management Plan and Environmental Impact Statement* (Draft). Prepared by the Boston Support Office of the Northeast Region, National Park Service for the Boston Harbor Islands Partnership. Boston, MA, 2000.

———. *Boston Harbor Islands, A National Park Area. General Management Plan.* Prepared by the Boston Support Office of the Northeast Region, National Park Service for the Boston Harbor Islands Partnership. Boston, MA. 2002.

———. *Boston Harbor Islands National Recreation Area—American Indian Issues.* Briefing statement from the Northeast Region of the National Park Service to the U.S. Department of Interior, May 1, 1998.

Randall, Debra. *Archeological Survey of the Proposed MDC Sludge Mananagement Plant, Deer Island, Massachusetts.* Prepared for the Metropolitan District Commission and Havens and Emerson, Inc., by the Institute for Conservation Archeology, Peabody Museum, Harvard University, Cambridge, MA., 1981.

Revolutionary War Bicentennial Commission. *Massachusetts in Ferment. The Coming of the American Revolution. A Chronological Survey, 1760–1775*, 1971.

Ritchie, Duncan, and Marsha King. *Deer Island, Boston Harbor, Massachusetts.* Prepared for the Massachusetts Water Resources Authority by the Public Archeology Laboratory, 1986.

ARTICLES

Adams, Jim. "Ghost of King Philip's War Haunts Boston Harbor Park." *Indian Country Today*, January 19, 2004.

Allen, Scott. "Rethinking Value of a Sparkling Harbor." *Boston Globe.* May 2, 1993.

———. "Scientists Recreate 1918 Flu Pandemic Virus." *Boston Globe*, October 6, 2005.

Andrew, Charles M. "A City Goes on the Alert." *Boston Globe*, September 22, 2001.

———. "Colonial Commerce." *Classics of American Colonial History. American Historical Review 20*, (October 1914): 43-63. http://www.dinsduc.com/andrews_1.htm, May 7, 2002.

Arnold, David. "Taking Out the Trash." *Boston Globe*, July 13, 2001.

Barquet, Nicolau, MD, and Pere Domingo, MD. "Smallpox: The Triumph over the Most Terrible of the Ministers of Death." *Annals of Internal Medicine*, 15 October 1997. 127: 636–642. American College of Physicians. http://www.acponline.org/journals/annals/15 oct97/

Billings, Molly. "The Pandemic of 1918." http://www.stanford.edu/group/virus/uda, February 2005.

Blake, Andrew. "Volunteer Finds 500 Military Artifacts on Georges Island." *Boston Globe*, November 25, 1976.

"B.P. Cheney Dies in Arizona Wilds." *New York Times*, June 10, 1942.

"Changing Tides: The Future of Boston Harbor." *Boston Globe Magazine* (special issue), November 3, 1985.

"Charles Solomon." http:// en.wikipedia.org/wiki/charles_solomon

Bibliography

Damon, Allen L. "The Great Red Scare." *American Heritage.* http://www.americanheritage. com/articles/magazine/ah/1968/2/1968_2_22.shtml.

Ebbert, Stephanie. "Opening of Island Park Again Delayed." *Boston Globe,* June 26, 2004.

Gaffin, Adam. "Boston Harbor." http://Boston-online.com/harbor, March 8,2002.

Holloway, Lee. "Ghosts of the Massachusetts Lights." http://www.prairieghosts.com/MA_ lights.html, May 25, 2005.

Howe, Peter J. "The Other Harbor Cleanup." *Boston Globe,* August 31, 1998.

"Julia Arthur, 81, Retired Actress." Special to the *New York Times,* March 30, 1950.

Kales, David. "The Islands of Boston Harbor." *Eastern Sea Magazine.* New York, NY: CBS Publications, July 1977.

Kenney, Michael. "Crediting the Court with Spurring Harbor Cleanup." *Boston Globe,* June 1, 2005.

Kolata, Gina. "Hazard in Hunt for New Flu: Looking for Bugs in all the Wrong Places." *New York Times,* November 8, 2005.

"Legislators Move to Lift Boston's Native American Ban." *News of Boston,* May 24, 2005. http://www 2.whdh.com/news/articles/local/DBB954/

MacQuarrie, Brian. "Spectacle Island Makeover Revives Connection to the Past." *Boston Sunday Globe,* January 2, 2005.

Murphy, Sean P. "Decision Day at Court for Nipmuc Indians." *The Boston Globe,* December 15, 2001.

———. "Nipmucs Become State's Second Recognized Tribe." *Boston Globe,* January 20, 2000.

Palmer, Louise. "The Moon Island Mambo." *Boston Magazine,* November 1995.

Palmer, Thomas C., Jr. "Offshore Access—Pipeline Plan to Help Fund Boston Harbor Islands Projects." *Boston Globe,* May 11, 2002.

Pogatchnik, Shawn. "Irish 'famine ship' Ready to Sail to U.S." *The Boston Globe,* February 13, 2003.

Rolbein, Seth. "Boston's Floating Crap Game." *Boston Magazine*, May 1987.

"Rum-running." http://www.answers.com/topics/rum-running.

Saltus, Richard. "How Boston Beat a Smallpox Epidemic." *Boston Globe, February 2, 2001.*

Scheindlin, Benjamin. "A Revolutionary in the Smallpox War." *Boston Globe Magazine*, May 11, 2003.

"The Second Engagement of the Revolutionary War." Description of the Battle of Chelsea Creek (Noddles Island). http://olgp.net/chs/war/second.htm.

Sege, Irene. "An Island out of Time." *Boston Globe*, August 13, 1998.

Shea, Lois. "Sudden, Swift, Silent and Deadly. 80 Years Ago, Flu Ravaged New England." *Boston Sunday Globe*, November 1, 1998.

Simon, Brona G. "Massachusetts Bay." *Highway to the Past: The Archeology of Boston's Big Dig.* Boston, MA: William Francis Gavin, Secretary of the Commonwealth; Chairman of the Massachusetts Historical Commission, 2001.

Slack, Donovan. "Indians Seeking Respect for the Deal at Last." *Boston Sunday Globe*, April 27, 2003.

Sullivan, Mark. "Letters Offer Link to Slave Trade." *Boston Globe*, March 14, 1999.

Taylor, Mia. "Indian Demanding MWRA Apology." *Quincy Patriot Ledger,* February 1, 2001.

Vallar, Cindy. "Pirates and Privateers. The History of Maritime Piracy." http://www.cindyvallar.com/privateers.html, 2003

Vasquez, Daniel, and Rob Nelson. "9 Miles into Tunnel, Air Ran out for 2." *Boston Globe*, July 22, 1999.

"Yet Another Site for Kidd's Treasure in Massachusetts." A letter attributed to Robert Kidd, University of Massachusetts. http://www.bio.umass.edu/biology/conn.river/palmer.html.

OTHER SOURCES

Boston Harbor Islands National Park Area. http://bostonislands.com.

———. Natural Resources Overview. *Northeastern Naturalist*, Vol. 12, Special Issue 3, 2005.

Bibliography

Boston Tea Party Ship and Museum. http://bostonteapartyship.com/history.htm.

"Chelsea Creek: A River Flowing through History." Brochure published by Riverways's Urban Rivers Program.

"Considerations for the future of Outer Brewster Island, Boston Harbor Islands." East Boston, Boston 200 Neighborhood History Series. Boston 200 Corporation, 1976.

Massachusetts Water Resources Authority newsletter. "Your Deer Island Tour," 1999.

Massport. "Logan International Airport Then and Now." http://www.massport.com/logan/about_histo.html, 1999.

Minutes of meetings of the Boston Harbor Islands Advisory Council, 2000–2006.

"National Park Area." Memo to Stephen Pritchard, secretary of Massachusetts Environmental Affairs, and Stephen Burrington, commissioner of the Department of Conservation and Recreation, from Bruce Jacobson, superintendent of Boston Harbor Islands National Park Area, November 15, 2005.

Nettler, John and Kane, Ryan. *The History of Recreation in the Boston Harbor Islands*, 1998. Research project for seminar, "Boston's Public Past," Boston University. http://www.bu.edu/history courses/hi 457/bhi-recreational historytitlepge.html. (NA)

INDEX

About the Author

David Kales has been a journalist, editor and freelance writer for over forty years. His journalist experience includes *Newsweek*, *Forbes*, *INC* and foreign correspondent for the Hearst Newspapers, covering the Vietnam War and Southeast Asia. He was also a recipient of a Carnegie Foundation grant, awarded by the Columbia School of Journalism, for reporting on China. He has written and edited numerous publications on business, international affairs and environmental/recreational matters. He is author of *All About the Boston Harbor Islands* (co-authored with his wife, Emily) and a novel, *The Phantom Pirate—Tales of the Irish Mafia and the Boston Harbor Islands.*

Please visit us at
www.historypress.net